DAY HIKES AROUND

Ventura County

82 GREAT HIKES

Robert Stone

2nd EDITION

Day Hike Books, Inc.

RED LODGE, MONTANA

Published by Day Hike Books, Inc.
P.O. Box 865
Red Lodge, Montana 59068

Distributed by The Globe Pequot Press
246 Goose Lane
P.O. Box 480
Guilford, CT 06437-0480
800-243-0495 (direct order) · 800-820-2329 (fax order)
www.globe-pequot.com

Photographs by Robert Stone
Design by Paula Doherty

The author has made every attempt to provide accurate information in this book. However, trail routes and features may change—please use common sense and forethought, and be mindful of your own capabilities. Let this book guide you, but be aware that each hiker assumes responsibility for their own safety. The author and publisher do not assume any responsibility for loss, damage, or injury caused through the use of this book.

Cover photo: Waterfall in Santa Paula Canyon, Hike 25.
Back cover photo: Paradise Falls, Hikes 60 and 61.

Table of Contents

About the Hikes and Ventura County 6
Map of the Hikes 8

THE HIKES
Summerland • Carpinteria
1. Summerland Beach: Lookout Park 10
2. Loon Point 12
3. Salt Marsh Nature Park 14
4. Tarpits Park 16
5. Carpinteria Bluffs and Seal Sanctuary 18
6. Rincon Point and Rincon Beach Park 20

Ojai • Santa Paula
Map of Ojai and Santa Paula (Hikes 7—25) 22
7. Potrero John Trail 24
8. Rose Valley Falls 26
9. Lion Canyon Trail to West Fork Lion Camp .28
10. Piedra Blanca Formations 30
11. Sespe River Trail 32
12. Wheeler Gorge Nature Trail 34
13. Murietta Canyon 36
14. Matilija Creek 38
15. Matilija Camp Trail 40
16. Cozy Dell Trail 42
17. Shelf Road 44
18. Stewart Canyon 46
19. Foothill Trail to Cozy Dell Canyon 48
20. Foothill Fire Road—Gridley Fire Road—Shelf Road Loop 50
21. Gridley Trail to Gridley Springs Camp 52
22. Horn Canyon Trail 54
23. Sulphur Mountain Road Recreation Trail 56
24. Sisar Canyon 58
25. Santa Paula Canyon 60

Ventura • Oxnard • Camarillo
Map of coastal hikes and Santa Monica Mountains (Hikes 26—50) 62
26. Ocean's Edge—River's Edge Loop
    Emma Wood State Beach • Seaside Wilderness Park 64

27. San Buenaventura State Beach
    to the Ventura River Estuary 65
28. Santa Clara Estuary Natural Preserve: McGrath State Beach 68
29. Arroyo Verde Park 70
30. Port Hueneme Beach Park 72
31. Bubbling Springs Recreational Greenbelt 74
32. Mission Oaks Community Park Trail 76

Santa Monica Mountains:
Point Mugu State Park • Circle X Ranch
Leo Carrillo State Beach • Rancho Sierra Vista/Satwiwa

33. Ranch Overlook Trail—Satwiwa Loop
    Rancho Sierra Vista/Satwiwa 78
34. Wendy—Satwiwa Loop Trail
    Rancho Sierra Vista/Satwiwa 79
35. Boney Mountain Trail to Sycamore Canyon Falls
    Rancho Sierra Vista/Satwiwa · Point Mugu State Park 82
36. Big Sycamore Canyon Trail: Point Mugu State Park 84
37. Chumash Trail—Mugu Peak Loop: Point Mugu State Park 86
38. La Jolla Valley Loop from La Jolla Canyon
    Point Mugu State Park 87
39. Scenic and Overlook Trails Loop: Point Mugu State Park 90
40. Grotto Trail: Circle X Ranch 92
41. Canyon View—Yerba Buena Road Loop: Circle X Ranch 94
42. Sandstone Peak Loop: Mishe Mokwa—Backbone Trails
    Circle X Ranch 96
43. Lower Arroyo Sequit Trail and Sequit Point
    Leo Carrillo State Beach 98
44. Nicholas Flat and Willow Creek Loop
    Leo Carrillo State Beach 100
45. Nicholas Flat: Leo Carrillo State Beach 102
46. Arroyo Sequit Park 104
47. Charmlee County Park 106
48. Newton Canyon Falls: Zuma/Trancas Canyons 108
49. Newton Canyon: Zuma/Trancas Canyons 110
50. Rocky Oaks Park 112

Thousand Oaks

Map of Thousand Oaks, Oak Park, and Agoura Hills (Hikes 51—72) 114
51. Los Robles Trail: Potrero Gate to Angel Vista 116
52. Los Robles Trail: Moorpark Gate to Angel Vista 117
53. Oak Creek Canyon: Los Robles Trail System 120

54. Los Padres—Los Robles Loop: Los Robles Trail System 122
55. White Horse Canyon Trail: Los Robles Trail System 124
56. Triunfo Canyon Trail: Los Robles Trail System 125
57. Dawn's Peak 128
58. Conejo Valley Botanic Garden 130
59. Lynnmere—Wildwood Canyon Loop (East Side)
    Wildwood Park 132
60. ᐧ Lynnmere—Arroyo Conejo—Wildwood Canyon Loop (West Side):
    Wildwood Park 133
61. Paradise Falls: Wildwood Park 136
62. Lizard Rock: Mesa—Stagecoach Bluff Loop
    Wildwood Park 138
63. Mountclef Ridge: Santa Rosa Trail—Lower Butte Loop
    Wildwood Park 140
64. Hillcrest Open Space Preserve: North Ranch Open Space 142
65. Sandstone Hills Trail: North Ranch Open Space 143

Oak Park • Agoura Hills

66. Oak Canyon Community Park 146
67. Medea Creek Park 148
68. China Flat Trail: Cheeseboro/Palo Comado Canyons 150
69. Palo Comado—Cheeseboro Canyons Loop
    Cheeseboro/Palo Comado Canyons 152
70. Cheeseboro Canyon to Shepherds' Flat
    Cheeseboro/Palo Comado Canyons 154
71. Canyon View—Cheeseboro Canyon Loop
    Cheeseboro/Palo Comado Canyons 156
72. Cheeseboro Ridge—Cheeseboro Canyon Loop
    Cheeseboro/Palo Comado Canyons 158

Fillmore • Moorpark • Simi Valley

Map of Fillmore, Moorpark, and Simi Valley (Hikes 73—82) 160
73. Tar Creek 162
74. Happy Canyon Camp 164
75. Mount McCoy 166
76. Chumash Trail: Rocky Peak Park 168
77. Hummingbird Trail: Rocky Peak Park 170
78. Rocky Peak Trail: Rocky Peak Park 172
79. Corriganville Park 174
80. Old Stagecoach Trail 176
81. Sage Ranch Loop Trail 178
82. Orcutt Ranch Horticulture Center 180

The Ventura County Area

Ventura County lies along the Pacific Coast between Los Angeles County and Santa Barbara County. The area has a Mediterranean-like climate, ideal for hiking year round. Ventura County has hundreds of miles of hiking trails across a very diverse landscape with unique geological features. The elevation dramatically changes from sea level to over 3,000 feet in the Santa Monica Mountain range, which runs parallel to the coast. A complex ecosystem and extensive wildlife habitat exists amidst the highly populated area. Large tracts of public lands, forests, and wilderness areas lie throughout the region, preserving major parcels of undeveloped land. Running through the county are the Santa Monica Mountains, the Simi Hills, The Santa Susana Mountains, and the Topatopa Mountains. The county is bounded to the north by the Los Padres National Forest.

Day Hikes Around Ventura County offers 82 of the best hikes in this scenic coastal country. A cross-section of scenery, geography, and difficulty levels is included to accommodate all ranges of hiking experience. Highlights include coastal estuaries and tidepools, long beaches backed by bluffs, expansive sand dunes, waterfalls, swimming holes, vine-entangled gorges, massive sandstone formations, caves, mountain meadows, ridge walks, historic sites, filming locations, and spectacular views. You may enjoy these areas for a short time or the whole day. A quick glance at the hikes' summaries will allow you to choose a trail that is appropriate to your ability and desire.

An overall map on the next page identifies the general locations of the hikes and major roads. Four area maps (outlined on the overall map) provide additional details. All hikes can be completed during the day and are within a half-hour's drive of Highway 101, the major access road.

Each hike also includes its own map, a summary, driving and hiking directions, and an overview of distance/time/elevation. Relevant maps, including U.S.G.S. topographic maps, are listed with each hike if you wish to explore more of the area.

Hikes 1—6 are all coastal hikes between Ventura and Santa

Barbara, just west of the Ventura County line. These six coast hikes include beach parks, tidepools, oceanside cliffs, forested trails, a large wetland, and a seal sanctuary.

Hikes 7—25 are found in the area around the city of Ojai. Nearly all of the hikes here travel along river valleys and canyons. The lightly used trails wind through national forests and wilderness land. This beautiful inland area includes several waterfalls, impressive sandstone ridges, and great views of the Ojai valley.

Hikes 26—32 are minutes from Ventura, yet offer solitude and beauty along protected stretches of coastline, rolling sand dunes, and metropolitan parks.

Hundreds of acres of public land and an impressive series of state parks are found between Ventura and Los Angeles in the Santa Monica Mountains. Hikes 33—50 travel across Point Mugu State Park, Rancho Sierra Vista/Satwiwa, Circle X Ranch, Leo Carrillo State Beach, the Zuma/Trancas Canyons, and several county parks.

The inland valleys and the Simi Hills are explored in hikes 51—72. The thoughtfully developed Los Robles Trail System links wide inland valleys with the Santa Monica Mountains. Wildwood Park is an immense park with a diverse ecosystem that includes waterfalls and rocky overlooks. Cheeseboro and Palo Comado Canyons run through former ranch land that is home to lush canyons, high grassy meadows, and 200-year-old twisted oaks.

The last ten trails, hikes 73—82, are also inland hikes in the Simi Hills and Simi Valley. Miles of trails run through abandoned ranch land composed of deep canyons, highland meadows, overlooks, and sculpted sandstone rock gardens and caves.

A few basic necessities will make your hike more enjoyable. Wear supportive, comfortable hiking shoes. Take along hats, sunscreen, sunglasses, drinking water, snacks, and appropriate outerwear. Poison oak and ticks are common in these areas. Exercise caution by using insect repellent and staying on the trails.

There is a range of sites and hikes from one end of Ventura County to the other. Enjoy hiking in this diverse and beautiful area!

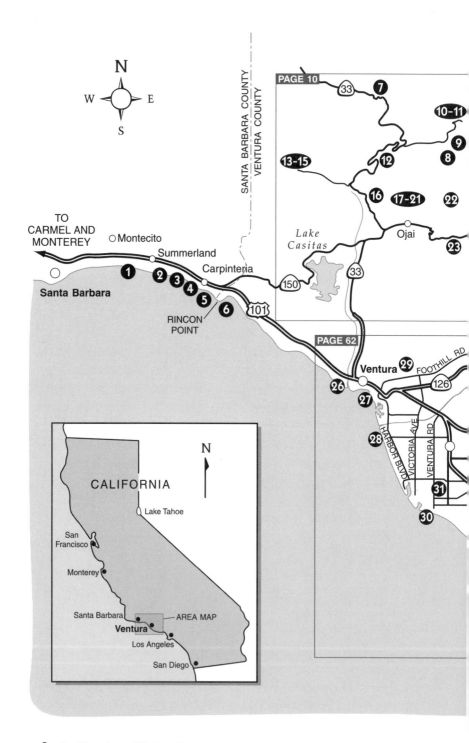

N
W E
S

PAGE 10

33 7

10-11

9

8

13-15 12

16 17-21 22

TO
CARMEL AND ○ Montecito
MONTEREY Summerland
Carpinteria

Lake
Casitas Ojai

23

○
Santa Barbara

1 2 3 4
5
6
RINCON
POINT 101

150 33

PAGE 62

Ventura 29 FOOTHILL RD
26 126
27

28 VICTORIA AVE VENTURA RD

31

30

CALIFORNIA N

Lake Tahoe

San
Francisco

Monterey

Santa Barbara AREA MAP
Ventura
Los Angeles

San Diego

SANTA BARBARA COUNTY
VENTURA COUNTY

MAP OF THE HIKES
VENTURA COUNTY and VICINITY

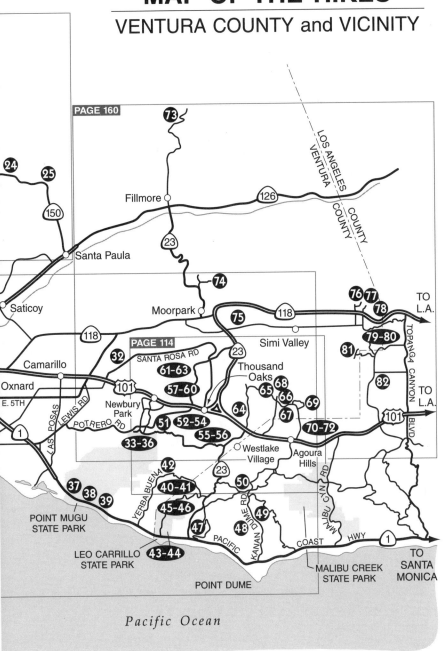

PAGE 160

73

24 25

Fillmore

126

150

23

Santa Paula

74

Saticoy

Moorpark

75

118

LOS ANGELES COUNTY
VENTURA COUNTY

76 77
78

TO L.A.

118

32

SANTA ROSA RD

23

Simi Valley

PAGE 114

61-63

57-60

Camarillo

101

Thousand Oaks

65 68
66

81

79-80

TOPANGA CANYON

82

TO L.A.

Oxnard

E. 5TH

Newbury Park

LEWIS RD

LAS POSAS

POTRERO RD

51 52-54

55-56

33-36

64

69

67

70-72

101

TO L.A.

1

Westlake Village

Agoura Hills

MALIBU CYN RD

42

40-41

45-46

37 38 39

YERBA BUENA

23

50

47

48

49

KANAN DUME RD

POINT MUGU
STATE PARK

LEO CARRILLO
STATE PARK

43-44

PACIFIC

POINT DUME

COAST HWY

1

MALIBU CREEK
STATE PARK

TO
SANTA
MONICA

Pacific Ocean

Hike 1
Summerland Beach
LOOKOUT PARK

Hiking distance: 1 mile loop
Hiking time: 30 minutes
Elevation gain: 50 feet
Maps: U.S.G.S. Carpinteria
   The Thomas Guide—Santa Barbara & Vicinity

Summary of hike: Lookout Park is a beautiful grassy flat along the oceanfront cliffs in Summerland. From the 4-acre park perched above the sea, paved walkways, and natural forested trails lead down to the sandy Summerland Beach, creating a one-mile loop. There are tidepools and coves a short distance up the coast from the beach.

Driving directions: From Ventura, drive northbound on Highway 101 to Summerland, and take the Evans Avenue exit. Turn left (south), cross under Highway 101 and over the railroad tracks, one block to Lookout Park. Park in the parking lot.
   From Santa Barbara, drive southbound on Highway 101 and take the Summerland exit. Turn right (south), crossing the railroad tracks in a block, and park in the Lookout Park parking lot.

Hiking directions: From the parking lot, head left (east) through the grassy flat along the cliff's edge to an open gate. A path leads through a shady eucalyptus forest. Cross a wooden bridge and head to the sandy shoreline. At the shore, bear to the right, leading to the paved walkways that return up to Lookout Park. To extend the hike, continue along the coastline to the west. At low tide, the long stretch of beach leads to coves, rocky points and tidepools.
   The beach continues west past charming beachfront homes, reaching Eucalyptus Lane and the Hammonds Meadow Trailhead at 2 miles. From Lookout Park, the beach heads 1.5 miles east to Loon Point (Hike 2).

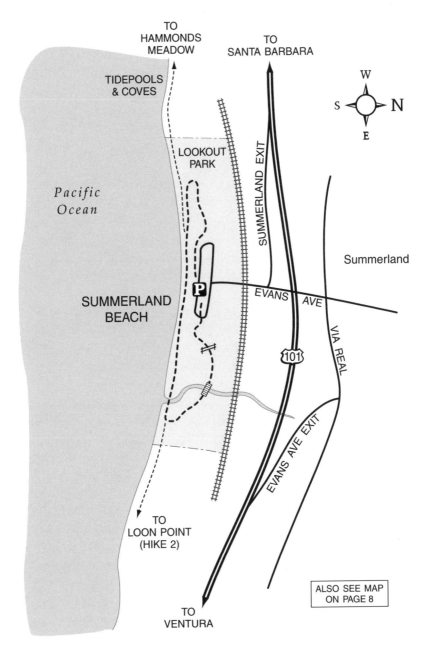

SUMMERLAND BEACH
LOOKOUT PARK

Hike 2
Loon Point

Hiking distance: 3 miles round trip
Hiking time: 1.5 hours
Elevation gain: Near level
Maps: U.S.G.S. Carpinteria
      The Thomas Guide—Santa Barbara and Vicinity

Summary of hike: Loon Point sits between Summerland and Carpinteria at the mouth of Toro Canyon Creek. Dense stands of sycamores, coastal oaks, Monterey cypress, and eucalyptus trees line the creek. The path to Loon Point follows an isolated stretch of coastline along the base of steep 40-foot sandstone cliffs.

Driving directions: From Ventura, drive northbound on Highway 101 to Summerland, and take the Padero Lane exit. Turn left on South Padero Lane, and drive 0.4 miles, crossing Highway 101 and curving east, to the signed Loon Point Beach parking lot on the left.

From Santa Barbara, drive southbound on Highway 101 to Summerland, and exit on Padero Lane south. Turn right and drive 0.2 miles to the signed Loon Point Beach parking lot on the left.

Hiking directions: Take the signed Loon Beach access trail parallel to the railroad tracks. Curve to the left, under the Padero Lane bridge and past a grove of eucalyptus trees. The path descends through a narrow drainage between the jagged weathered cliffs to the shoreline. Bear to the right on the sandy beach along the base of the sandstone cliffs. Loon Point can be seen jutting out to sea. Follow the shoreline, reaching large boulders at Loon Point in 1.5 miles. At high tide, the water level may be too high to reach the point. At low tide, the beach walk can be extended from Loon Point to Lookout Park, 1.5 miles west (Hike 1).

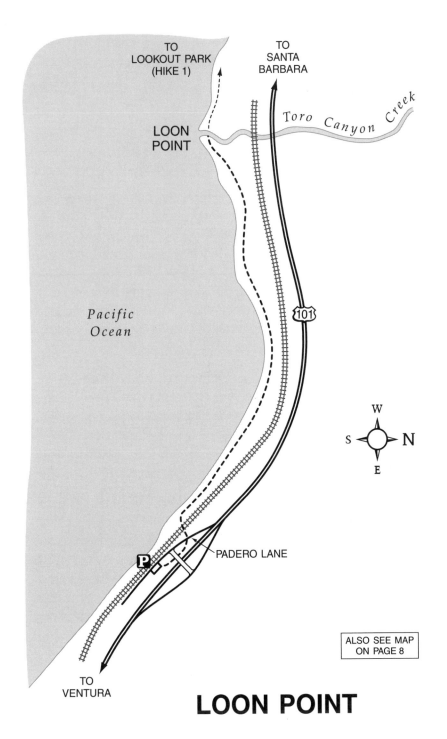

TO
LOOKOUT PARK
(HIKE 1)

TO
SANTA
BARBARA

Toro Canyon Creek

LOON
POINT

Pacific
Ocean

101

W
S — N
E

PADERO LANE

P

ALSO SEE MAP
ON PAGE 8

TO
VENTURA

LOON POINT

Hike 3
Salt Marsh Nature Park

Hiking distance: 1 mile round trip
Hiking time: 30 minutes
Elevation gain: Level
Maps: U.S.G.S. Carpinteria
  The Thomas Guide—Santa Barbara and Vicinity

Summary of hike: The Carpinteria Salt Marsh, historically known as El Estero (the estuary), is one of California's last remaining wetlands. The area was once inhabited by Chumash Indians. The 230-acre marsh is fed by Franklin Creek and Santa Monica Creek. The marsh has an abundance of sea and plant life and is a nesting ground for thousands of migratory waterfowl and shorebirds. The Salt Marsh Nature Park sits along the east end of the salt marsh with a trail system and several observation decks.

Driving directions: From Ventura, drive northbound on Highway 101 to Carpinteria, and exit on Linden Avenue. Drive 0.6 miles south on Linden Avenue to Sandyland Road, the last corner before reaching the ocean. Turn right and continue 0.2 miles to Ash Avenue. Park alongside the road by the signed park.

Hiking directions: From the nature trail sign, walk 20 yards to the west, reaching an observation deck. A boardwalk to the left leads to the ocean. Take the wide, meandering path to the right, parallel to Ash Avenue and the salt marsh. At the north end of the park, curve left to another overlook of the wetland. At the T-junction, the left fork leads a short distance to another observation deck. The right fork follows a pole fence along Franklin Creek to the trail's end. Return along the same path.

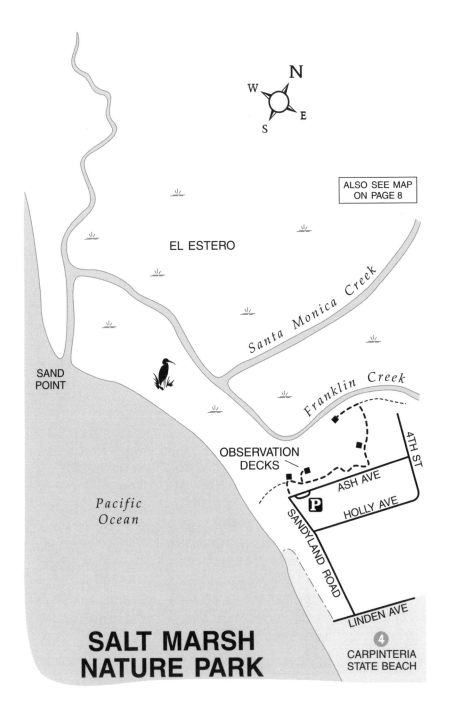

N
W E
S

ALSO SEE MAP ON PAGE 8

EL ESTERO

Santa Monica Creek

Franklin Creek

SAND POINT

OBSERVATION DECKS

4TH ST

ASH AVE

P

HOLLY AVE

SANDYLAND ROAD

Pacific Ocean

LINDEN AVE

4 CARPINTERIA STATE BEACH

SALT MARSH NATURE PARK

Hike 4
Tarpits Park

Hiking distance: 1.5 miles round trip
Hiking time: 1 hour
Elevation gain: 50 feet
Maps: U.S.G.S. Carpinteria

Summary of hike: Tarpits Park is an 8-acre blufftop park at the east end of Carpinteria State Beach. The park was once the site of a Chumash Indian village. It is named for the natural tar that seeps up from beneath the soil. The Indians used the tar for caulking canoes and sealing cooking vessels. Interconnecting trails cross the bluffs overlooking the steep, jagged coastline. Benches are placed along the edge of the bluffs.

Driving directions: From Ventura, drive northbound on Highway 101 to Carpinteria, and exit on Linden Avenue. Turn right and drive 0.5 miles south on Linden Avenue to Sixth Street. Turn left and go 0.2 miles to Palm Avenue. Turn right and drive one block to the Carpinteria State Beach parking lot on the right. A parking fee is required.

Hiking directions: Two routes lead to Tarpits Park. Either follow the sandy beach east, or walk along the campground road east, crossing over Carpinteria Creek. At a half mile, the campground road ends on the grassy bluffs. From the beach, a footpath ascends the bluffs to the campground road. Several interconnecting paths cross the clifftop terrace. The meandering trails pass groves of eucalyptus trees and Monterey pines. A stairway leads down to the shoreline. As you near the Chevron Oil Pier, the bluffs narrow. This is a good turnaround spot.

To hike further, cross the ravine and continue past the pier along the edge of the cliffs. You will reach the Carpinteria Bluffs and Seal Sanctuary (Hike 5) in a half mile.

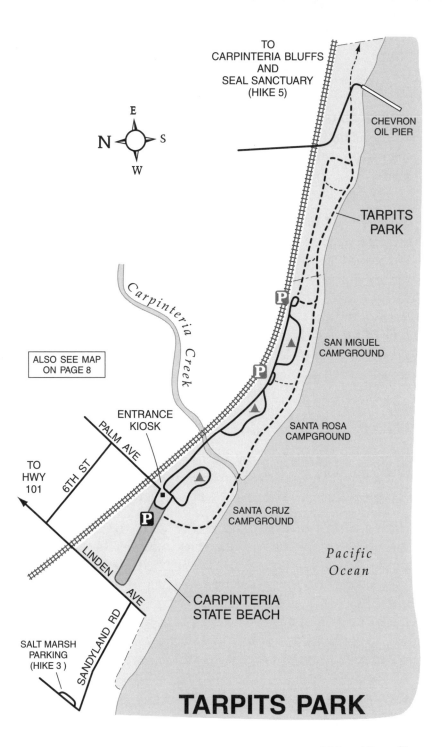

TO
CARPINTERIA BLUFFS
AND
SEAL SANCTUARY
(HIKE 5)

CHEVRON
OIL PIER

E
N S
W

TARPITS
PARK

Carpinteria Creek

ALSO SEE MAP
ON PAGE 8

San MIGUEL
CAMPGROUND

ENTRANCE
KIOSK

PALM AVE

6TH ST

TO
HWY
101

SANTA ROSA
CAMPGROUND

P

SANTA CRUZ
CAMPGROUND

Pacific
Ocean

LINDEN AVE

SANDYLAND RD

CARPINTERIA
STATE BEACH

SALT MARSH
PARKING
(HIKE 3)

TARPITS PARK

Hike 5
Carpinteria Bluffs
and Seal Sanctuary

Hiking distance: 2 miles round trip
Hiking time: 1 hour
Elevation gain: Level
Maps: U.S.G.S. White Ledge Peak and Carpinteria
　　　　The Thomas Guide—Santa Barbara & Vicinity

Summary of hike: The Carpinteria Bluffs and Seal Sanctuary are located in an incredible area along the Pacific. The bluffs encompass 52 oceanside acres with grasslands and eucalyptus groves. The area has panoramic views from the Santa Ynez Mountains to the islands of Anacapa, Santa Cruz, and Santa Rosa. At the cliff's edge, 100 feet above the ocean, is an over-look of the seal sanctuary. Below, a community of harbor seals plays in the water, lounging, and sunbathing on the rocks and shoreline. The sanctuary is a protected birthing habitat for harbor seals during the winter and spring from December 1 through May 31. Beach access is prohibited during these months, but the seals may be watched from the blufftop.

Driving directions: From Ventura, drive northbound on Highway 101 to Carpinteria, and exit on Bailard Avenue. Drive one block south towards the ocean, and park at the road's end.

Hiking directions: From the end of the road, hike south on the well-worn path across the open meadow towards the ocean. As you near the ocean cliffs, take the pathway to the right, parallel to a row of stately eucalyptus trees. At the west end of the eucalyptus grove, bear left and cross the railroad tracks. The trail resumes across the tracks, heading to the right. (For an optional side trip, take the beach access trail on the left down to the base of the cliffs.) Continue west along the edge of the ocean bluffs to a bamboo fence—the seal sanctuary overlook. After enjoying the seals and views, return along the same path.

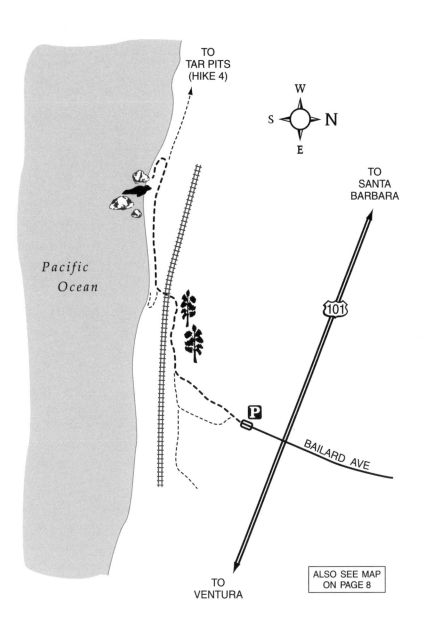

TO
TAR PITS
(HIKE 4)

W
S —◇— N
E

TO
SANTA
BARBARA

Pacific
Ocean

101

P

BAILARD AVE

TO
VENTURA

ALSO SEE MAP
ON PAGE 8

CARPINTERIA BLUFFS
AND
SEAL SANCTUARY

Hike 6
Rincon Point and Rincon Beach Park

Hiking distance: 2 miles round trip
Hiking time: 1 hour
Elevation gain: 100 feet
Maps: U.S.G.S. White Ledge Peak
　　　　The Thomas Guide—Santa Barbara and Vicinity

Summary of hike: Rincon Point is a popular surfing spot with tidepools and a small bay. Rincon Beach Park is on the west side of the point. The park sits on the steep, forested bluff with eucalyptus trees and Monterey pines. There is a large picnic area, great views of the coastline, and a stairway to the 1,200 feet of beach frontage.

Driving directions: From Ventura, drive northbound on Highway 101 to the Ventura—Santa Barbara county line, and take the Bates Road exit. Turn left and cross Highway 101 one block to the parking lots. Park in the lots on either side of Bates Road.

From Santa Barbara, drive southbound on Highway 101. Continue 3 miles past Carpinteria, and take the Bates Road exit to the stop sign. Turn right, and park in the lots on either side of Bates Road.

Hiking directions: Begin from the Rincon Park parking lot on the right (west). From the edge of the cliffs, a long staircase and a paved service road both lead down the cliff face, providing access to the sandy shoreline and tidepools. Walk north along the beach, strolling past a series of tidepools along the base of the sandstone cliffs. After beachcombing, return to the parking lot. From the west end of the parking lot, a well-defined trail heads west past the metal gate. The path is a wide shelf cut on the steep cliffs high above the ocean. At 0.3 miles, the trail reaches the railroad tracks. The path parallels the railroad right-of-way west to Carpinteria. Choose your own turnaround spot.

From the Rincon Point parking lot on the east, take the wide beach access path. Descend through a shady, forested grove to the beach. Bear right on the rocky path to a small bay near the tree-lined point. This is an excellent area to explore the tidepools and watch the surfers. Return the way you came.

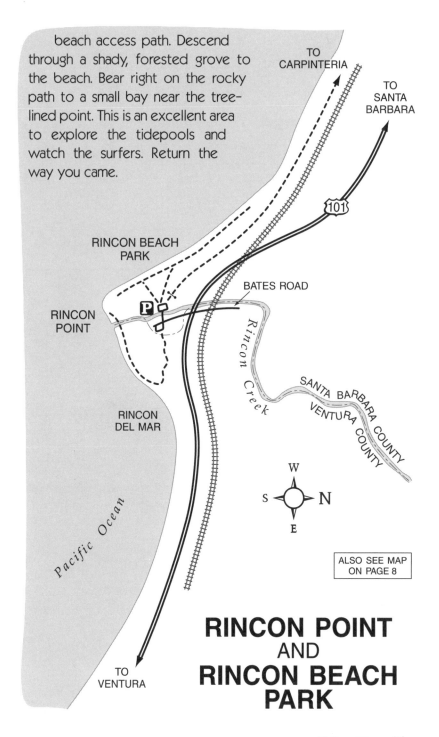

TO CARPINTERIA

TO SANTA BARBARA

101

RINCON BEACH PARK

BATES ROAD

RINCON POINT

P

RINCON DEL MAR

Rincon Creek

SANTA BARBARA COUNTY

VENTURA COUNTY

W

S —⬥— N

E

Pacific Ocean

ALSO SEE MAP ON PAGE 8

TO VENTURA

RINCON POINT
AND
RINCON BEACH PARK

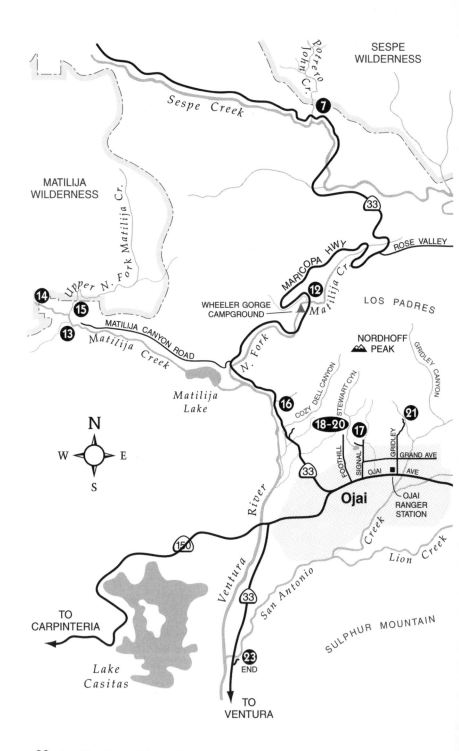

SESPE
WILDERNESS

MATILIJA
WILDERNESS

Potrero John Cr.

Sespe Creek

7

Upper N. Fork Matilija Cr.

N. Fork Matilija Cr.

MARICOPA HWY

33

ROSE VALLEY

Matilija Cr.

LOS PADRES

14

15

13

MATILIJA CANYON ROAD

WHEELER GORGE
CAMPGROUND

12

Matilija Creek

N. Fork

NORDHOFF
PEAK

GRIDLEY CANYON

Matilija
Lake

COZY DELL CANYON

STEWART CYN

16

21

N

W   E

S

33

18-20

17

FOOTHILL

SIGNAL

GRIDLEY

GRAND AVE

OJAI   AVE

Ojai

OJAI
RANGER
STATION

River

Creek

150

Lion Creek

Ventura

San Antonio

TO
CARPINTERIA

33

SULPHUR MOUNTAIN

Lake
Casitas

23
END

TO
VENTURA

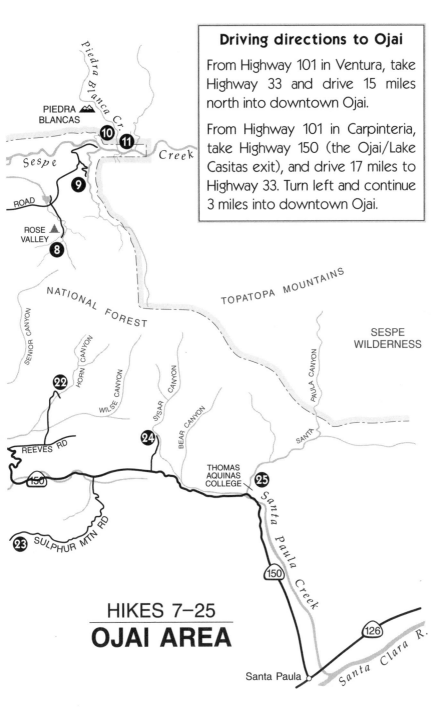

PIEDRA
BLANCAS

10
11

Piedra Blanca Cr.

Sespe

Creek

ROAD

9

ROSE
VALLEY

8

Driving directions to Ojai

From Highway 101 in Ventura, take Highway 33 and drive 15 miles north into downtown Ojai.

From Highway 101 in Carpinteria, take Highway 150 (the Ojai/Lake Casitas exit), and drive 17 miles to Highway 33. Turn left and continue 3 miles into downtown Ojai.

NATIONAL FOREST

TOPATOPA MOUNTAINS

SESPE
WILDERNESS

SENIOR CANYON

HORN CANYON

WILSE CANYON

SISAR CANYON

BEAR CANYON

PAULA CANYON

SANTA

22

24

REEVES RD

150

23

SULPHUR MTN RD

THOMAS
AQUINAS
COLLEGE

25

Santa Paula Creek

150

126

HIKES 7–25
OJAI AREA

Santa Paula

Santa Clara R.

Hike 7
Potrero John Trail

Hiking distance: 4 miles round trip
Hiking time: 2 hours
Elevation gain: 600 feet
Maps: U.S.G.S. Wheeler Springs
       Sespe Wilderness Trail Map

Summary of hike: The Potrero John Trail is an uncrowded, lightly used trail in the 220,000-acre Sespe Wilderness, part of the Los Padres National Forest. The hike begins at an elevation of 3,655 feet, where Potrero John Creek empties into Sespe Creek. The trail follows Potrero John Creek through a narrow gorge and up the canyon. There is also an open meadow dotted with red baked manzanita and views of the surrounding mountains. At the trail's end is Potrero John Camp, a creekside flat shaded with oaks.

Driving directions: From Ojai, drive 21 miles north on Highway 33 (Maricopa Highway) to the trailhead parking pullout on the right side of the road. It is located on the north side of Potrero Bridge.

Hiking directions: Hike north past the trailhead sign, immediately entering the narrow, steep-walled canyon on the west side of Potrero John Creek. After three successive creek crossings, the trail enters the Sespe Wilderness. There are eight creek crossings in the first mile while passing various pools and cascades. At one mile, the trail leaves the narrow canyon, emerging into a large, open meadow. At the far side of the meadow, the trail ends at Potrero John Camp, a walk-in camp on the banks of the creek. To return, retrace your steps.

To hike further, a rough, unmaintained trail heads upstream over rocks, underbrush, and downfall. Along the way there are continuous pools, cascades, and small waterfalls.

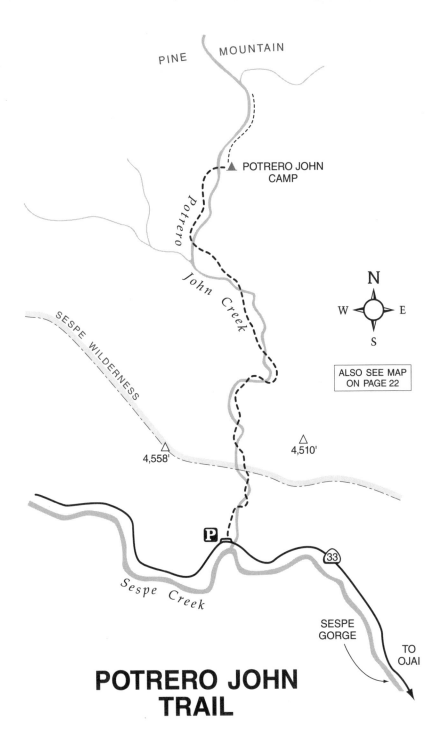

PINE MOUNTAIN

▲ POTRERO JOHN
CAMP

Potrero

John Creek

SESPE WILDERNESS

N
W ☆ E
S

ALSO SEE MAP
ON PAGE 22

△
4,558'

△
4,510'

P

33

Sespe Creek

SESPE
GORGE

TO
OJAI

POTRERO JOHN
TRAIL

Hike 8
Rose Valley Falls

Hiking distance: 0.8 miles round trip
Hiking time: 30 minutes
Elevation gain: 300 feet
Maps: U.S.G.S. Lion Canyon
　　　　　Sespe Wilderness Trail Map

Summary of hike: Rose Valley Falls is a 300-foot, two-tiered waterfall. This hike follows Rose Valley Creek up a shady canyon to the base of the lower falls, a 100-foot, multi-strand waterfall. The waterfall cascades over the sheer sandstone cliffs onto the rocks below in a cool, moss covered grotto. This short, easy trail begins at the Rose Valley Campground at an elevation of 3,450 feet. There are also three lakes near the campground that are stocked with trout.

Driving directions: From Ojai, drive 14.6 miles north on Highway 33 (Maricopa Highway) to the Rose Valley turnoff and turn right. Continue 3 miles to the Rose Valley Campground turnoff across from the lower lake and turn right. Drive 0.6 miles to the south end of the campground loop road to the signed trailhead by campsite number 4.

Hiking directions: Hike south past the trailhead sign, immediately entering the thick oak, bay, and sycamore forest on the well-defined trail. Cross the creek and stay on the main path as you make your way up the lush, narrow canyon. The first of several small waterfalls can be spotted on the left at 0.2 miles. Short side paths lead down to the creek by these waterfalls and pools. The trail ends in less than a half mile at the base of lower Rose Valley Falls with its bridal veil beauty. Return along the same path.

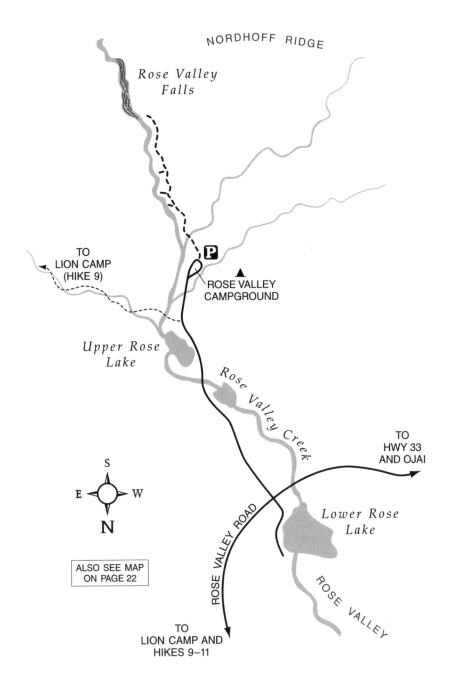

NORDHOFF RIDGE

Rose Valley Falls

TO
LION CAMP
(HIKE 9)

P

▲
ROSE VALLEY
CAMPGROUND

Upper Rose Lake

Rose Valley Creek

TO
HWY 33
AND OJAI

S
E ✦ W
N

ALSO SEE MAP
ON PAGE 22

Lower Rose Lake

ROSE VALLEY ROAD

ROSE VALLEY

TO
LION CAMP AND
HIKES 9–11

ROSE VALLEY FALLS

Hike 9
Lion Canyon Trail
to West Fork Lion Camp

Hiking distance: 5 miles round trip
Hiking time: 2.5 hours
Elevation gain: 350 feet
Maps: U.S.G.S. Lion Canyon
       Sespe Wilderness Trail Map

Summary of hike: The West Fork Lion Camp sits along the banks of the creek on a shady flat. Minutes beyond the camp is a beautiful waterfall and deep pool surrounded by rocks. The trail to the camp heads up the forested Lion Canyon parallel to Lion Canyon Creek.

Driving directions: From Ojai, drive 14.6 miles north on Highway 33 (Maricopa Highway) to the Rose Valley turnoff and turn right. Continue 4.8 miles to a road split. Take the right fork 0.8 miles down to the Middle Lion Campground and trailhead parking area.

Hiking directions: Walk east along the unpaved campground road, crossing Lion Canyon Creek. Take the signed trail to the right, and head south up Lion Canyon. Continue hiking gradually uphill along the east side of the canyon. At 1.3 miles is a posted junction with the Rose-Lion Connector Trail to the right (Hike 8). Proceed straight ahead, staying in Lion Canyon, to another creek crossing at two miles. After crossing is a three-way trail split known as Four Points Trail Junction. To the left, 0.5 miles ahead, is East Fork Lion Camp and a waterfall that lies within the Sespe Wilderness. Straight ahead is the steep trail up to Nordhoff Ridge. Take the right fork and stay on the east side of the creek along the edge of the rocky hillside. Less than a half mile from the junction is the West Fork Lion Camp. Rock hop up the narrow drainage a short distance past the camp to a beautiful waterfall and pool. Return by retracing your steps.

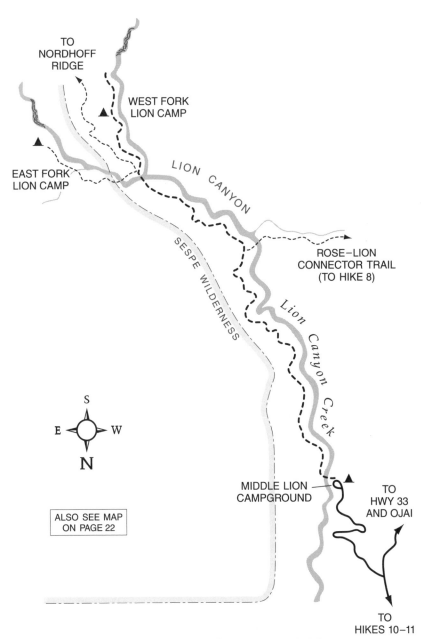

TO
NORDHOFF
RIDGE

WEST FORK
LION CAMP

EAST FORK
LION CAMP

LION CANYON

SESPE WILDERNESS

ROSE–LION
CONNECTOR TRAIL
(TO HIKE 8)

Lion Canyon Creek

S

E —◇— W

N

ALSO SEE MAP
ON PAGE 22

MIDDLE LION
CAMPGROUND

TO
HWY 33
AND OJAI

TO
HIKES 10–11

LION CANYON TRAIL
TO WEST FORK LION CAMP

Hike 10
Piedra Blanca Formations

GENE MARSHALL—PIEDRA BLANCA NATIONAL RECREATION TRAIL

Hiking distance: 2.5 miles round trip
Hiking time: 1.5 hours
Elevation gain: 300 feet
Maps: U.S.G.S. Lion Canyon
        Sespe Wilderness Trail Map

Summary of hike: The magnificent Piedra Blanca Formations in the Sespe Wilderness are huge, white rounded sandstone outcroppings sculpted by wind and water. The Gene Marshall-Piedra Blanca National Recreation Trail leads past these massive formations. You can easily spend the day exploring the trails around the unique rocks, cavities, and caves.

Driving directions: From Ojai, drive 14.6 miles north on Highway 33 (Maricopa Highway) to the Rose Valley turnoff and turn right. Continue 4.8 miles to a road split. Take the left fork one mile down to the Lion Campground and trailhead parking lot at the road's end along the banks of Sespe Creek.

Hiking directions: Rock hop across wide Sespe Creek. Continue to the trailhead sign and trail junction. The right fork is the Sespe River Trail (Hike 11). Take the left fork, heading north towards Piedra Blanca Camp. The trail crosses through chaparral hills past a creekbed to another junction. The left fork heads west towards Howard Creek and Beaver Campground. Proceed to the right, entering the Sespe Wilderness, towards the prominent Piedra Blanca formations. At the formations, leave the main trail and explore the area, choosing your own route. Return along the main trail back to the trailhead.

    To hike further, the trail continues north, descending into a small canyon and across a stream. The trail parallels Piedra Blanca Creek up canyon to Piedra Blanca Camp at 2.4 miles. Twin Forks Camp is a half mile further.

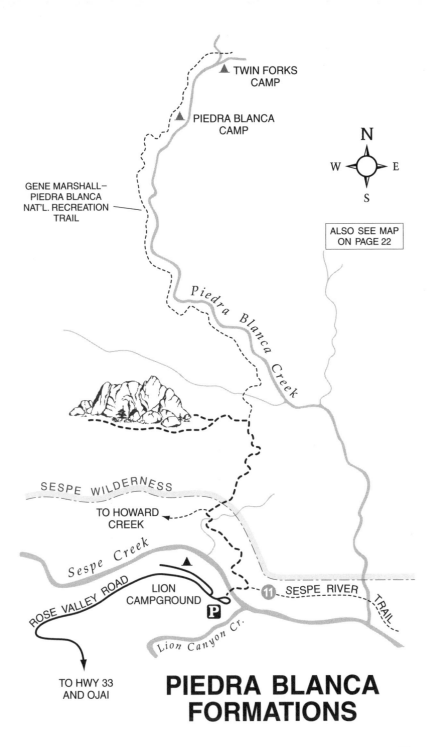

TWIN FORKS
CAMP

PIEDRA BLANCA
CAMP

N

W ✦ E

S

GENE MARSHALL–
PIEDRA BLANCA
NAT'L. RECREATION
TRAIL

ALSO SEE MAP
ON PAGE 22

Piedra Blanca Creek

SESPE WILDERNESS

TO HOWARD
CREEK

Sespe Creek

LION
CAMPGROUND

ROSE VALLEY ROAD

P

11 SESPE RIVER

TRAIL

Lion Canyon Cr.

TO HWY 33
AND OJAI

PIEDRA BLANCA
FORMATIONS

Hike 11
Sespe River Trail

Hiking distance: 3.5 miles round trip
Hiking time: 2 hours
Elevation gain: 200 feet
Maps: U.S.G.S. Lion Canyon
Sespe Wilderness Trail Map

Summary of hike: Sespe Creek is a wide body of water that appears more like a river than a creek. This hike follows a portion of the Old Sespe Road into the Sespe Wilderness to a scenic overlook. The trail parallels the creek past deep pools and sandy flats, crossing Piedra Blanca and Trout Creeks. The 18-mile Old Sespe Road eventually leads to Sespe Hot Springs.

Driving directions: From Ojai, drive 14.6 miles north on Highway 33 (Maricopa Highway) to the Rose Valley turnoff and turn right. Continue 4.8 miles to a road split. Take the left fork one mile down to the Lion Campground and trailhead parking area at the road's end.

Hiking directions: Cross Sespe Creek and the rocky creekbed, heading north to the posted trail junction. The left fork leads to the Piedra Blanca formations (Hike 10). Take the right fork and head downstream, parallel to the northern banks of Sespe Creek. In a half mile, the trail crosses Piedra Blanca Creek. After crossing, the trail narrows as it enters a canyon. Past the canyon, the trail widens out again and crosses Trout Creek. Along the way, side paths lead down to the creek. A short distance ahead, the trail enters the Sespe Wilderness. The trail gains elevation to a vista overlooking the canyon and passes through a gate. At the top of the ridge, the view opens up to the mountains in the north. The ridge is the turnaround spot.

To hike further, the trail follows Sespe Creek downstream for miles with numerous creek crossings. The first crossing is at Bear Canyon, 4.5 miles from the trailhead.

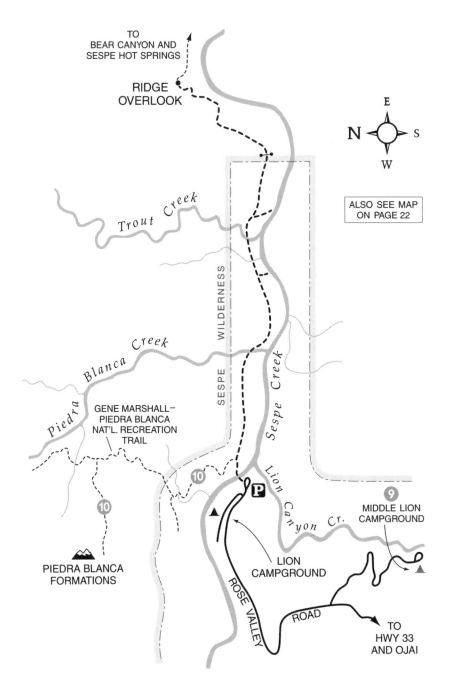

TO
BEAR CANYON AND
SESPE HOT SPRINGS

RIDGE
OVERLOOK

E
N ◇ S
W

ALSO SEE MAP
ON PAGE 22

Trout Creek

SESPE WILDERNESS

Piedra Blanca Creek

Sespe Creek

GENE MARSHALL–
PIEDRA BLANCA
NAT'L. RECREATION
TRAIL

Lion Canyon Cr.

10

P

10

MIDDLE LION
CAMPGROUND
9

PIEDRA BLANCA
FORMATIONS

LION
CAMPGROUND

ROSE VALLEY ROAD

TO
HWY 33
AND OJAI

SESPE RIVER TRAIL

Hike 12
Wheeler Gorge Nature Trail

Hiking distance: 1 mile loop
Hiking time: 30 minutes
Elevation gain: 200 feet
Maps: U.S.G.S. Wheeler Springs
Sespe Wilderness Trail Map

Summary of hike: Wheeler Gorge Nature Trail is an interpretive trail on the North Fork Matilija Creek near Wheeler Gorge Campground. The trail is an excellent introduction to the shaded creekside riparian habitats and arid chaparral plant communities that are so common throughout the area. The path winds through a small canyon gorge under sycamores, cottonwoods, willows, and oaks, following the year-round creek past trickling waterfalls and bedrock pools. Free brochures from the Ojai Ranger Station correspond with numbered posts along the trail.

Driving directions: From Ojai, drive 8 miles north on Highway 33 (Maricopa Highway) to the Wheeler Gorge Campground on the left. Continue on the highway 0.5 miles to the posted nature trail on the left by a locked metal gate, just before crossing the bridge over the North Fork Matilija Creek.

Hiking directions: From the trailhead map panel, take the path to the right, following the North Fork Matilija Creek upstream. Cross under the Highway 33 bridge, passing cascades, small waterfalls, and pools. Rock hop to the north side of the creek, and climb up through chaparral dotted with oaks. Follow the watercourse, passing a 12-foot waterfall between signposts 7 and 8. Cross over a rock formation, and wind through a shady tunnel of tall chaparral. Climb rock steps to a vista of Dry Lakes Ridge to the north. Curve away from the creekside vegetation, and descend on the northern slope of the arid hillside. Curve left and parallel Highway 33 from above. Drop back down to the creek, completing the loop. Recross the creek and return to the trailhead.

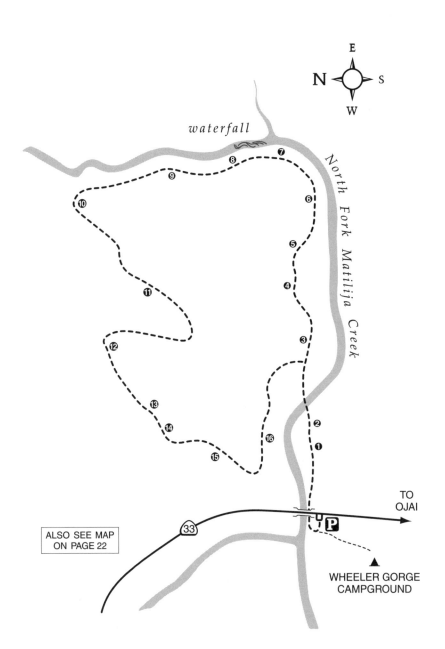

WHEELER GORGE
NATURE TRAIL

Hike 13
Murietta Canyon

Hiking distance: 3 miles round trip
Hiking time: 1.5 hours
Elevation gain: 200 feet
Maps: U.S.G.S. Old Man Mountain and White Ledge Peak

Summary of hike: The Murietta Trail begins in Matilija Canyon and enters Murietta Canyon en route. The trail follows Murietta Creek while heading to a campground on a beautiful, wooded flat. Murietta Camp sits at the edge of Murietta Creek under a forest canopy dominated by cedar and oak trees. There are cascades and pools at the creek.

Driving directions: From Ojai, drive 4.9 miles north on Highway 33 (Maricopa Highway) to Matilija Canyon Road and turn left. Continue 4.8 miles to the parking area on the left by the trailhead gate.

Hiking directions: From the parking area, follow the road past the gate and trailhead sign. Continue west along the unpaved road, crossing two streams. At 0.7 miles, a short distance past the second stream, is the signed Murietta Trail on the left. Leave the road and head south on the footpath towards the mouth of Murietta Canyon. Proceed to a stream crossing by pools and cascades. Rock hop across the stream channels and up a small hill, heading deeper into the canyon. Murietta Camp is at 1.7 miles. From the camp, several trails lead down to the stream. Return along the same path.

Up the canyon from the campground, the trail enters a dense forest with a tangle of vegetation and underbrush. This unmaintained trail becomes vague and hard to follow.

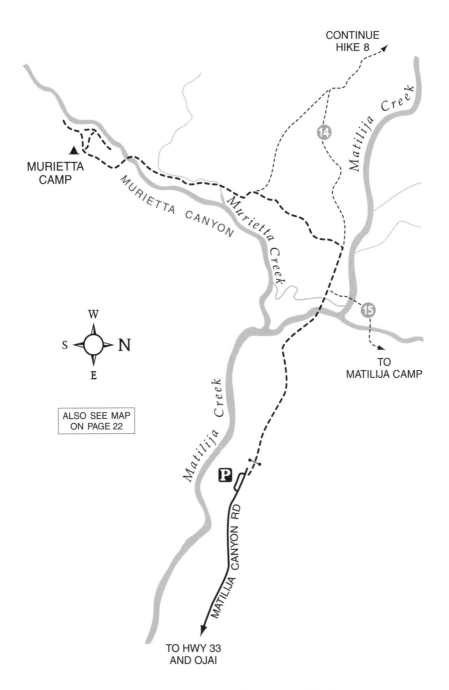

CONTINUE
HIKE 8

Matilija Creek

14

MURIETTA
CAMP

MURIETTA CANYON

Murietta Creek

W
S N
E

15

TO
MATILIJA CAMP

ALSO SEE MAP
ON PAGE 22

Matilija Creek

P

MATILIJA CANYON RD

TO HWY 33
AND OJAI

MURIETTA CANYON

Hike 14
Matilija Creek

Hiking distance: 7 miles round trip
Hiking time: 3 hours
Elevation gain: 600 feet
Maps: U.S.G.S. Old Man Mountain

Summary of hike: Matilija Creek leads up the main canyon to beautiful pools, cascades, and water slides. Large shale slabs border the creek for sunbathing beneath the steep canyon cliffs. Up canyon are several towering waterfalls.

Driving directions: From Ojai, drive 4.9 miles north on Highway 33 (Maricopa Highway) to Matilija Canyon Road and turn left. Continue 4.8 miles to the parking area on the left by the trailhead gate.

Hiking directions: Hike west up the road, past the gate and across two streams. Stay on the main road to an intersection with another trail at one mile. Take the right fork past a house on a Forest Service easement. For a short distance, the trail borders a beautiful rock wall. As you approach the mountain range, cross the stream and curve to the right. The trail follows the western edge of the deep, narrow canyon and crosses another stream. Climb up a short hill to a perch overlooking the canyon. Take the left fork that curves around the gully, and hike down the rocky drainage. Near the canyon floor, the trail picks up again to the left. Hike parallel to the creek along its endless cascades, pools, and rock slabs. This natural playground is the destination. Return along the same path.

To hike further, continue up canyon, creating your own path. There are several waterfalls ahead. Two are located another mile up the main canyon. Another falls is in the canyon to the northeast. This part of the hike is difficult due to slippery shale and an indistinct trail.

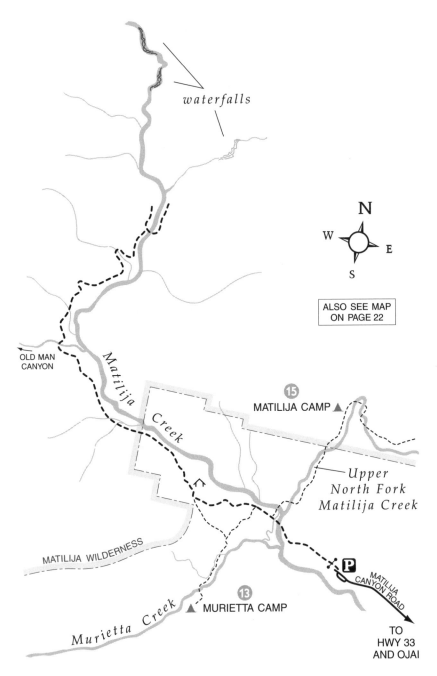

waterfalls

N
W + E
S

ALSO SEE MAP
ON PAGE 22

OLD MAN
CANYON

Matilija

Creek

15 MATILIJA CAMP ▲

*Upper
North Fork
Matilija Creek*

MATILIJA WILDERNESS

P

MATILIJA
CANYON ROAD

13 ▲ MURIETTA CAMP

Murietta Creek

TO
HWY 33
AND OJAI

MATILIJA CREEK

Hike 15
Matilija Camp Trail

Hiking distance: 2 miles round trip
Hiking time: 1 hour
Elevation gain: 200 feet
Maps: U.S.G.S. Old Man Mountain and Wheeler Springs

Summary of hike: The Matilija Camp Trail parallels the Upper North Fork of Matilija Creek in the Los Padres National Forest. The easy trail winds through the lush canyon in the shade of oaks and sycamores. There are three creek crossings en route to the Matilija Campsite, the destination for this hike. At the oak-shaded camp are large boulders, sandstone cliffs, swimming holes, pools, and a picnic area.

Driving directions: From Ojai, drive 4.9 miles north on Highway 33 (Maricopa Highway) to Matilija Canyon Road and turn left. Continue 4.8 miles to the parking area on the left by the trailhead gate.

Hiking directions: From the parking area, walk up the unpaved road past the gate, a wildlife refuge, and two creek crossings. At 0.5 miles, just past the second creek crossing, leave the road and take the signed Matilija Camp Trail to the right. The well-defined trail heads north, winding its way up the narrow canyon floor between steep, brown cliffs. Cross to the east side of the Upper North Fork Matilija Creek, entering the Matilija Wilderness. Matilija Camp and the pools are between the next two creek crossings. The camp is our turnaround spot.

   To hike further, the trail leads to Middle Matilija Camp in another two miles. The trail to the middle camp has several more creek crossings and passes through a wide meadow.

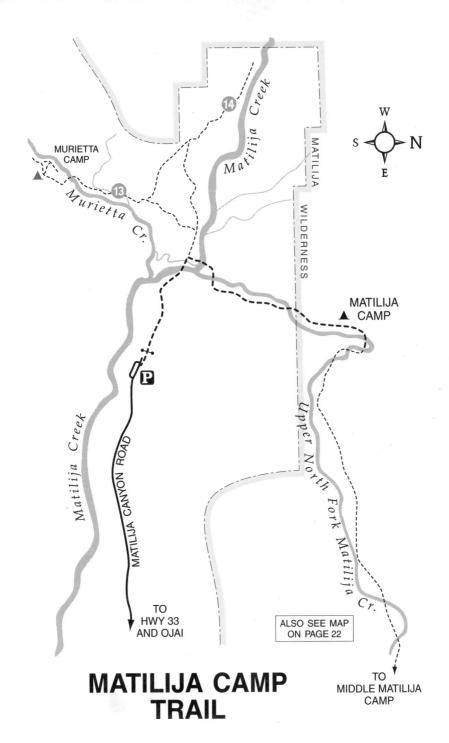

MATILIJA CREEK
WILDERNESS

W N S E

MURIETTA
CAMP

Murietta Cr.

Matilija Creek

14

Matilija Creek

MATILIJA

13

MATILIJA
CAMP

P

MATILIJA CANYON ROAD

Upper North Fork Matilija Cr.

TO
HWY 33
AND OJAI

ALSO SEE MAP
ON PAGE 22

TO
MIDDLE MATILIJA
CAMP

MATILIJA CAMP
TRAIL

Hike 16
Cozy Dell Trail

Hiking distance: 4 miles round trip
Hiking time: 2 hours
Elevation gain: 700 feet
Maps: U.S.G.S. Matilija
   Sespe Wilderness Trail Map

Summary of hike: The Cozy Dell Trail climbs up a small, shaded canyon to several vista points with panoramic views in every direction. There are great views into the Ojai Valley to the south and the surrounding peaks of the Santa Ynez and Topatopa Mountains. From the overlooks, the trail drops into the beautiful and forested Cozy Dell Canyon.

Driving directions: From Ojai, drive 3.4 miles north on Highway 33 (Maricopa Highway) to the Cozy Dell trailhead parking pullout on the left (west) side of the road. The pullout is located by a bridge, a packing house, and a Forest Service trailhead sign.

Hiking directions: From the parking area, cross the highway to the trailhead, south of the packing house along the right side of the metal railing. Take the well-defined trail east and head up the canyon. A short distance ahead is a series of 18 switchbacks, gaining 600 feet up the south edge of the canyon. At one mile, the trail reaches its peak at a saddle, giving way to an open area with breathtaking views. Proceed downhill towards Cozy Dell Canyon and back up to a second saddle with more outstanding views. The trail drops back into the trees, descending 200 feet into forested Cozy Dell Canyon, Cozy Dell Creek, and a T-junction with the Cozy Dell Road. One hundred yards to the left is a posted junction with the Foothill Trail (Hike 19). This is the turnaround spot. Return by retracing your steps.

To hike further, the fire road continues to the Pratt Trail and Foothill Fire Road at Stewart Canyon (Hikes 18—20).

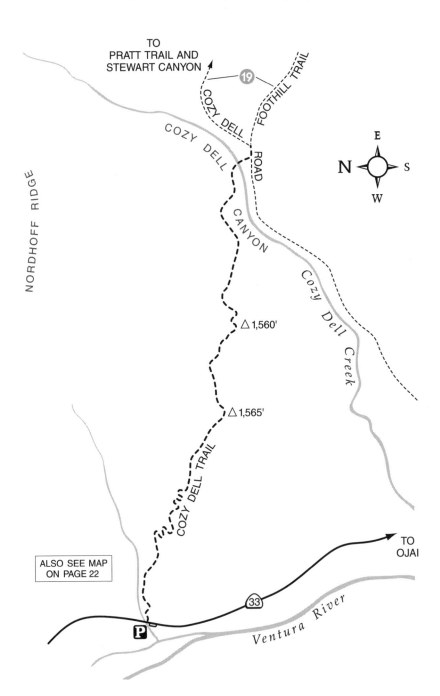

TO
PRATT TRAIL AND
STEWART CANYON

19

COZY DELL

FOOTHILL TRAIL

COZY DELL

ROAD

NORDHOFF RIDGE

CANYON

Cozy Dell Creek

△ 1,560'

△ 1,565'

COZY DELL TRAIL

ALSO SEE MAP
ON PAGE 22

TO
OJAI

P

33

Ventura River

COZY DELL TRAIL

Hike 17
Shelf Road

Hiking distance: 3.5 miles round trip
Hiking time: 1.5 hours
Elevation gain: 200 feet
Maps: U.S.G.S. Ojai
       Sespe Wilderness Trail Map

Summary of hike: Shelf Road is an old, unpaved road that traverses the cliffs several hundred feet above the northern edge of Ojai. The road, connecting Signal Street with Gridley Road, is gated at both ends. It is a hiking, biking, and jogging path that is popular with locals. The path has several scenic overlooks with views of the ten-mile long Ojai Valley, Sulphur Mountain across the valley, and the city of Ojai.

Driving directions: From downtown Ojai, drive one mile north up Signal Street (on the west side of the arcade) to the trailhead gate. Park along the side of the road.

Hiking directions: Hike north past the gate and up the abandoned road. The road curves east, passing orange trees and avocado groves. Shelf Road follows the contours of the cliffs, snaking its way to the east above the city. At 1.7 miles, the trail ends at another entrance gate by Gridley Road. Return to the trailhead along the same route.

For a longer hike, the Shelf Road hike may be combined with the Foothill-Gridley Loop (Hike 20). This loop hike is a backcountry hike while Shelf Road is more of an easy social stroll.

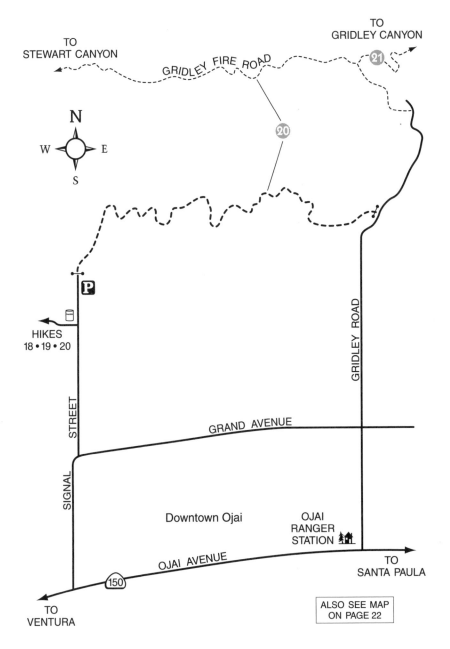

TO
STEWART CANYON

TO
GRIDLEY CANYON

GRIDLEY FIRE ROAD

21

20

N
W E
S

P

HIKES
18 • 19 • 20

GRIDLEY ROAD

STREET

SIGNAL

GRAND AVENUE

Downtown Ojai

OJAI
RANGER
STATION

OJAI AVENUE

150

TO
SANTA PAULA

TO
VENTURA

ALSO SEE MAP
ON PAGE 22

SHELF ROAD

Hike 18
Stewart Canyon

Hiking distance: 2.6 miles round trip
Hiking time: 1.5 hours
Elevation gain: 600 feet
Maps: U.S.G.S. Ojai and Matilija
       Sespe Wilderness Trail Map

Summary of hike: Stewart Canyon, at the north edge of Ojai, is the gateway to a network of magnificent hiking trails in the Los Padres National Forest. The canyon connects with the Foothill Trail to Cozy Dell Canyon (Hike 19), the Pratt Trail to Nordhoff Ridge, and the Gridley Fire Road to Gridley Canyon (Hike 20). This hike winds up the lower canyon, following Stewart Creek through a eucalyptus grove, meadows, and landscaped rock gardens to a scenic vista across the Ojai Valley.

Driving directions: From downtown Ojai, drive 0.8 miles north up Signal Street (on the west side of the arcade) to the Pratt/Foothill Trailhead sign by the water tower. Turn left and drive 0.2 miles to the parking area on the left.

Hiking directions: Take the posted Pratt Trail, and curve north up Stewart Canyon. Parallel Stewart Creek to an unpaved road and junction. Continue straight ahead, following the trail sign. Weave through boulders on the distinct trail to a second junction. Take the left fork and walk through a eucalyptus grove, heading up the east wall of Stewart Canyon. At one mile, the trail reaches a plateau above the canyon with great views of the Ojai Valley. Descend into the canyon, staying on the trail past a few hillside homes, a creekside rock garden, and a paved road crossing. Cross Stewart Creek and take the Foothill Fire Road to the right, following the "trail" signs. Continue along a beautiful rock wall. Pass a gate and water tank to the posted Pratt and Foothill Trail junction on the left (Hike 19). Stay on the main trail, and continue climbing a quarter mile to a Y-fork on a wide, rounded flat. This is our turnaround spot. The Gridley Fire

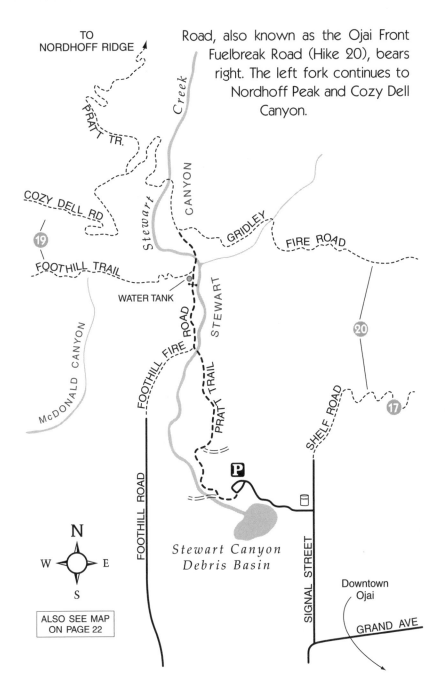

Road, also known as the Ojai Front Fuelbreak Road (Hike 20), bears right. The left fork continues to Nordhoff Peak and Cozy Dell Canyon.

TO NORDHOFF RIDGE

PRATT TR.

Creek

COZY DELL RD

CANYON

Stewart

GRIDLEY

FIRE ROAD

19

FOOTHILL TRAIL

WATER TANK

STEWART

FOOTHILL FIRE ROAD

PRATT TRAIL

20

McDONALD CANYON

SHELF ROAD

17

P

N
W — E
S

FOOTHILL ROAD

Stewart Canyon
Debris Basin

SIGNAL STREET

Downtown Ojai

GRAND AVE

ALSO SEE MAP
ON PAGE 22

STEWART CANYON

Hike 19
Foothill Trail to Cozy Dell Canyon

Hiking distance: 5.8 mile loop
Hiking time: 3 hours
Elevation gain: 1,200 feet
Maps: U.S.G.S. Ojai and Matilija
        Sespe Wilderness Trail Map

Summary of hike: This loop hike follows Stewart Creek up the canyon, passing meadows and rock gardens to the Foothill Trail. The route heads west through McDonald Canyon and drops into pastoral Cozy Dell Canyon by the creek. Cozy Dell Road winds up the forested canyon, climbing to sweeping overlooks beneath Nordhoff Peak.

Driving directions: From downtown Ojai, drive 0.8 miles north up Signal Street (on the west side of the arcade) to the Pratt/Foothill Trailhead sign by the water tower. Turn left and drive 0.2 miles to the parking area on the left.

Hiking directions: Follow the hiking directions up Stewart Canyon—Hike 18—to the posted Pratt and Foothill Trail junction by the water tank. Begin the loop to the left and climb rock steps, ascending the east-facing hillside to a trail split. Curve left and continue uphill along short switchbacks. There are great views down Stewart Canyon and across Ojai Canyon to Sulphur Mountain. Cross a saddle to views of Lake Casitas and the Santa Ynez Mountains. Drop into McDonald Canyon and cross another saddle. Descend a sloping meadow bordered by oaks. Head into Cozy Dell Canyon to the Cozy Dell Road. (A hundred yards to the left is the Cozy Dell Trail—Hike 16.) Bear right on the fire road towards the posted Pratt Trail, meandering through the rolling forested glen. Steadily climb out of the canyon to a junction on a saddle. Bear left and continue uphill, curving right around the mountain to a posted junction with the Pratt Trail to Nordhoff Peak. Stay on the fire road to the right, and head downhill into Stewart Canyon to an open flat and road split. The left fork is the Gridley Fire Road (Hike 20). Descend to the right a quarter mile and complete the loop. Return down Stewart Canyon to the trailhead.

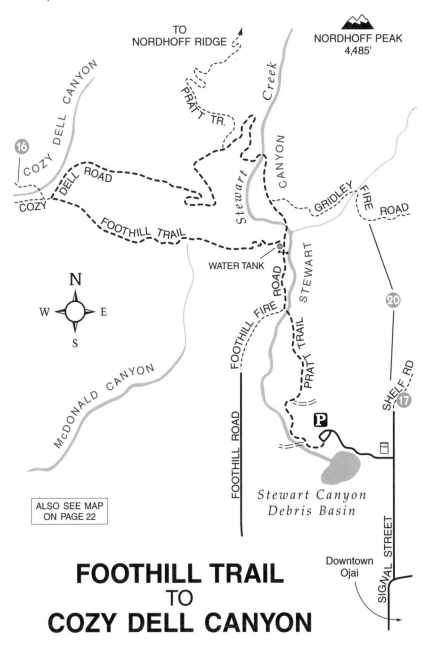

ALSO SEE MAP
ON PAGE 22

FOOTHILL TRAIL
TO
COZY DELL CANYON

Hike 20
Foothill Fire Road—Gridley Fire Road—Shelf Road Loop

Hiking distance: 6.4 mile loop
Hiking time: 3.5 hours
Elevation gain: 900 feet
Maps: U.S.G.S. Ojai and Matilija
  Sespe Wilderness Trail Map

Summary of hike: The Gridley Fire Road (Ojai Front Fuel-break Road) runs parallel to the Ojai Valley with stunning views a thousand feet above Ojai. The fire road connects Stewart Canyon on the west with Gridley Canyon on the east. This hike climbs up Stewart Canyon, traverses across the folded mountain layers to Gridley Road, and returns along Shelf Road. These fire roads are vehicle restricted.

Driving directions: From downtown Ojai, drive 0.8 miles north up Signal Street (on the west side of the arcade) to the Pratt/Foothill Trailhead sign by the water tower. Turn left and drive 0.2 miles to the parking area on the left.

Hiking directions: Follow the hiking directions for Hike 18 to the Gridley Fire Road junction—the turnaround point for Hike 18. At the junction, the left fork continues to Nordhoff Peak and Cozy Dell Canyon. Curve right on the Gridley Fire Road, and traverse the hillside on a winding course through the folded hills. Continue zigzagging eastward to a trail gate and posted junction on the right. The Gridley Trail (Hike 21) continues on the road to the left. Take the footpath to the right, and descend 0.4 miles to the top of Gridley Road. Follow Gridley Road downhill 0.3 miles to the Shelf Road trailhead on the right. Take Shelf Road and head west 1.7 miles to the Signal Street gate. The trailhead turnoff is 0.2 miles ahead by the water tower.

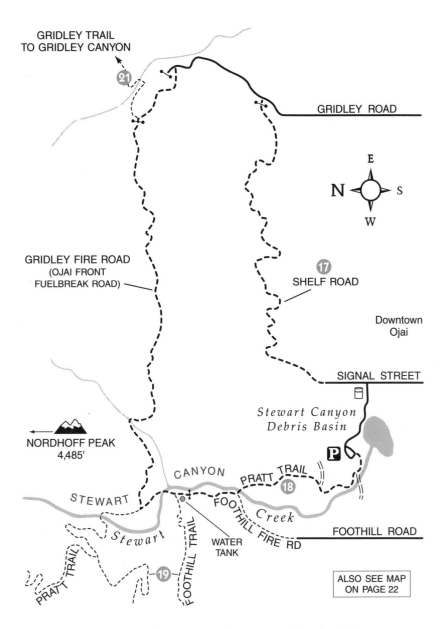

GRIDLEY TRAIL
TO GRIDLEY CANYON

㉑

GRIDLEY ROAD

E
N ✦ S
W

GRIDLEY FIRE ROAD
(OJAI FRONT
FUELBREAK ROAD)

⑰
SHELF ROAD

Downtown
Ojai

SIGNAL STREET

Stewart Canyon
Debris Basin

NORDHOFF PEAK
4,485'

P

CANYON

PRATT TRAIL
⑱

STEWART

FOOTHILL FIRE RD

Creek

FOOTHILL ROAD

Stewart

FOOTHILL TRAIL

WATER
TANK

PRATT TRAIL

⑲

ALSO SEE MAP
ON PAGE 22

FOOTHILL FIRE ROAD
GRIDLEY FIRE ROAD
SHELF ROAD

Hike 21
Gridley Trail
to Gridley Springs Camp

Hiking distance: 6 miles round trip
Hiking time: 3 hours
Elevation gain: 1,200 feet
Maps: U.S.G.S. Ojai
Sespe Wilderness Trail Map

Summary of hike: The Gridley Trail begins at the edge of Ojai in the foothills of the Topatopa Mountains. The trail follows a fire road into Gridley Canyon along the shady northwest side. Gridley Trail eventually leads six miles up to Nordhoff Peak. This hike goes to Gridley Springs Camp, a primitive campsite by a stream that is halfway to the peak.

Driving directions: From downtown Ojai, drive one mile east on Highway 150 (Ojai Avenue) to Gridley Road and turn left. Continue 1.5 miles to the end of Gridley Road, and park by the signed trailhead on the left.

Hiking directions: Take the signed trail on the west up a draw through the tall, native brush. Continue 0.4 miles to the Gridley Fire Road (Hike 20). There is a beautiful overlook of the Ojai Valley and Sulphur Mountain on the right. Head to the right up the unpaved, vehicle-restricted fire road past avocado orchards on the steep slopes. The road curves around the contours of the mountain to a signed five-way junction in Gridley Canyon. Take the center left fork, following the trail sign. At two miles, the trail is perched high above the deep canyon and enters a small side canyon at the confluence of two streams. Gridley Springs Camp is at the first sharp switchback by a horse watering trough. This is the turnaround spot.

To hike further, the trail continues up switchbacks for three steep miles, gaining over 2,000 feet to Nordhoff Peak.

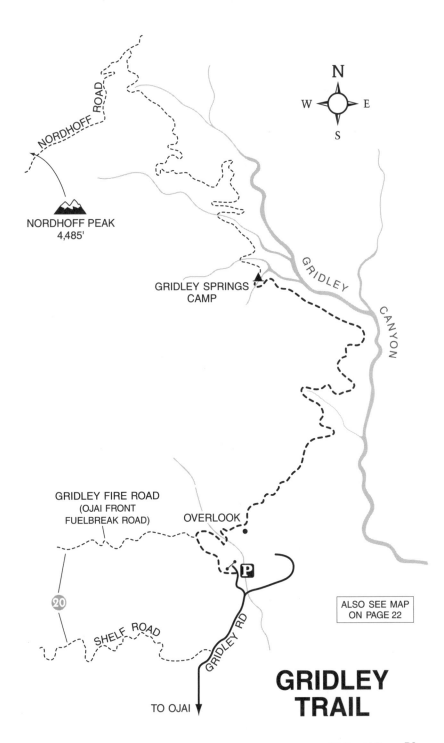

NORDHOFF ROAD

NORDHOFF PEAK
4,485'

GRIDLEY SPRINGS
CAMP

GRIDLEY CANYON

N
W E
S

GRIDLEY FIRE ROAD
(OJAI FRONT
FUELBREAK ROAD)

OVERLOOK

P

20

SHELF ROAD

GRIDLEY RD

TO OJAI

ALSO SEE MAP
ON PAGE 22

GRIDLEY TRAIL

Hike 22
Horn Canyon Trail

Hiking distance: 3 miles round trip
Hiking time: 1.5 hours
Elevation gain: 600 feet
Maps: U.S.G.S. Ojai
              Sespe Wilderness Trail Map

Summary of hike: The Horn Canyon Trail parallels Thacher Creek through a forested canyon that is lush with sycamores, alders, and oaks. The trail, which is partially a service road, crosses the creek four times to a rocky gorge. At the gorge, the trail is rugged and far less used, leading past a continuous series of cascades, pools, and small waterfalls.

Driving directions: From downtown Ojai, drive 2.3 miles east on Highway 150 (Ojai Avenue) to Reeves Road and turn left. Continue 1.1 mile to McAndrew Road and turn left again. Drive one mile and enter the Thacher School grounds. The trailhead parking area is 0.4 miles ahead, bearing right at all three road splits.

Hiking directions: From the parking area, take the unpaved service road northeast past the gate and kiosk into Horn Canyon. There are two creek crossings in the first half mile. After the second crossing, the service road enters the forest and the trail narrows. At one mile, the trail crosses the creek again and climbs up the west wall of the canyon. There are great views of Horn Canyon and the creek below. Just before the fourth creek crossing, leave the main trail and take the left path, heading up Horn Canyon along the west side of the creek. The trail is replaced by faint paths that crisscross the creek in a scramble past pools, cascades, and small waterfalls. Choose your own turnaround spot, and return along the same path.

To hike further, at the fourth creek crossing, continue on the Horn Canyon Trail across the creek. The trail steeply climbs out of the canyon to the Pines Campsite one mile ahead.

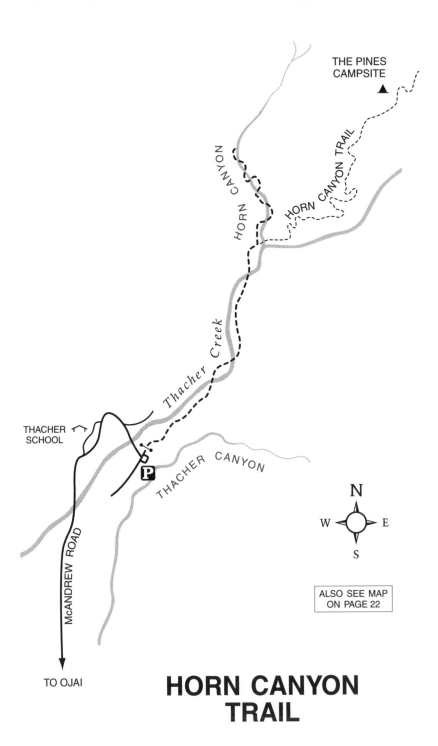

THE PINES
CAMPSITE
▲

HORN CANYON

HORN CANYON TRAIL

Thacher Creek

THACHER
SCHOOL

THACHER CANYON

P

McANDREW ROAD

TO OJAI

N
W   E
S

ALSO SEE MAP
ON PAGE 22

HORN CANYON
TRAIL

Hike 23
Sulphur Mountain Road Recreation Trail

Hiking distance: 10 miles one way (shuttle)
Hiking time: 4 hours
Elevation loss: 2,200 feet
Maps: U.S.G.S. Ojai and Matilija
　　　　 Sespe Wilderness Trail Map

Summary of hike: Sulphur Mountain Road, a gated hiking, biking and equestrian road, follows a 2,600-foot ridge along Sulphur Mountain. This hike is a downhill walk from the trailhead to the shuttle car. The journey across the ridgeline has gorgeous alternating views. There are views to the south and west of the Conejo Valley, the Pacific Ocean, and the Channel Islands. At other times there are views to the north of the Ojai Valley, the Topatopa Mountains, and the Los Padres National Forest.

Driving directions: Leave a shuttle car at the end of the hike: From Highway 101 in Ventura, drive 7.5 miles north on Highway 33 towards Ojai to Sulphur Mountain Road. Turn right and continue 0.4 miles to the locked gate. Park the shuttle car alongside the road.

　　To the trailhead: Return to Highway 33 and continue north to Ojai. From downtown Ojai, drive 6.4 miles east on Highway 150 towards Santa Paula. Turn right on Sulphur Mountain Road, and continue 4.6 miles up the winding road to a locked gate at the trailhead.

Hiking directions: From the locked gate, hike west along the paved road. At about 1.5 miles, the pavement ends. Continue west along the gradual but steady downhill trail along the mountain ridge. The last two miles are steeper, dropping 1,500 feet. As you near the trail's end, the winding road descends past a cattle guard and gate to the shuttle car parking area at Casitas Springs.

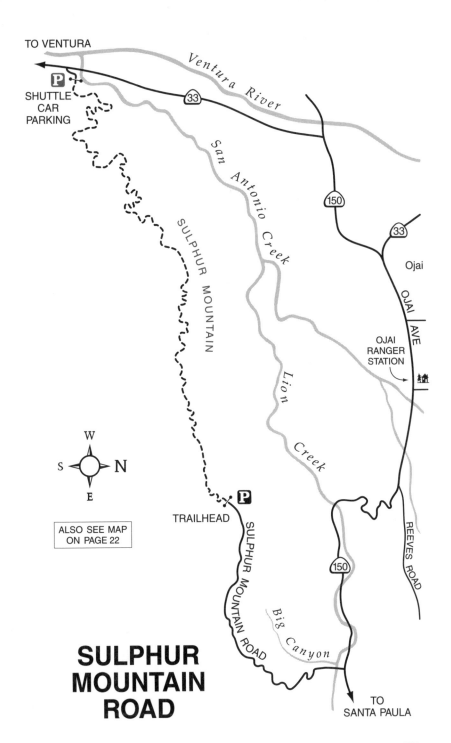

TO VENTURA

Ventura River

33

SHUTTLE
CAR
PARKING

San Antonio Creek

SULPHUR MOUNTAIN

150

33

Ojai

OJAI AVE

OJAI
RANGER
STATION

Lion Creek

W
N
S
E

ALSO SEE MAP
ON PAGE 22

TRAILHEAD

SULPHUR MOUNTAIN ROAD

REEVES ROAD

150

Big Canyon

SULPHUR
MOUNTAIN
ROAD

TO
SANTA PAULA

Hike 24
Sisar Canyon

Hiking distance: 4 miles round trip
Hiking time: 2 hours
Elevation gain: 1,000 feet
Maps: U.S.G.S. Ojai & Santa Paula Peak
        Sespe Wilderness Trail Map

Summary of hike: Sisar Canyon begins in the Upper Ojai Valley, halfway between Ojai and Santa Paula. The Sisar Canyon Trail follows Sisar Creek through a canopy of oak, sycamore, and bay laurel trees up this beautiful canyon. The hike involves two stream crossings and a scenic overlook with views across the Ojai Valley to Sulphur Mountain.

Driving directions: From downtown Ojai, drive 7.8 miles east towards Santa Paula on Highway 150. Turn left on Sisar Road along the eastern side of Summit School. Drive one mile to the trailhead gate, bearing right at the road split. Park on the side of the road.

From Santa Paula, drive 8.7 miles northwest on Highway 150 towards Ojai. Turn right on Sisar Road.

Hiking directions: Hike north past the trailhead gate up the fire road. Sisar Creek is to the right of the road. Within minutes, the trail crosses the creek by small waterfalls and pools. The trail steadily gains elevation up Sisar Canyon. At one mile, recross Sisar Creek. Continue up canyon, parallel to the creek, to a sharp left bend in the trail. The trail leaves the creek and begins to climb out of the canyon to an overlook and another switchback curving to the right. The overlook is the turnaround point for this hike. To return, follow the same trail back.

To hike further, the trail continues up the ridge for 3.5 miles to White Ledge Camp, eventually crossing the Topatopa Ridge into the Sespe Wilderness.

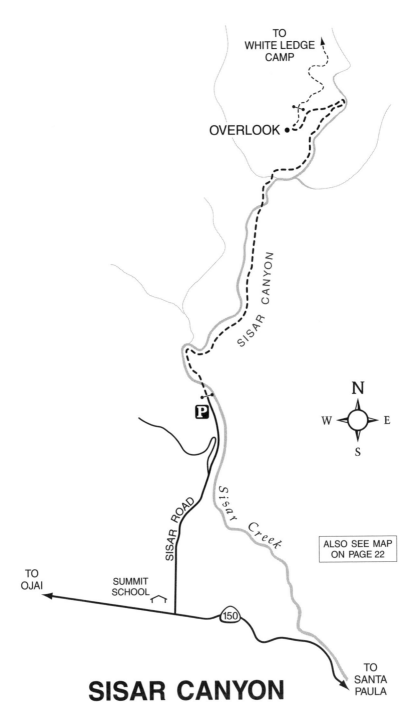

TO
WHITE LEDGE
CAMP

OVERLOOK ●

SISAR CANYON

N

W — E

S

P

Sisar Creek

SISAR ROAD

ALSO SEE MAP
ON PAGE 22

TO
OJAI

SUMMIT
SCHOOL

150

TO
SANTA
PAULA

SISAR CANYON

Hike 25
Santa Paula Canyon

Hiking distance: 6—8 miles round trip
Hiking time: 3—4 hours
Elevation gain: 750—900 feet
Maps: U.S.G.S. Santa Paula Peak
Sespe Wilderness Trail Map

Summary of hike: The Santa Paula Canyon Trail is among the most beautiful and popular hikes in the Ojai area. The trail follows Santa Paula Creek up a shady, forested canyon past a number of deep bedrock pools. The trail leads to The Punchbowl, a scenic, narrow gorge with waterfalls and pools (cover photo) between Big Cone Camp and Cross Camp.

Driving directions: From downtown Ojai, drive 11 miles east on Highway 150 towards Santa Paula. Park in the trailhead parking area on the right side of the road, just east of the bridge over Santa Paula Creek. The parking area is across from Thomas Aquinas College.

From Santa Paula, drive 5.7 miles northwest on Highway 150 towards Ojai. Park in the trailhead parking area on the left side of the road.

Hiking directions: From the trailhead parking lot, hike 500 feet up and across the road, entering Thomas Aquinas College. Stay on the paved road, heading north towards the far end of the campus. Near the top, take the road veering off to the right. Walk through the gate and past Ferndale Ranch. The road ends in front of two scenic oil rigs. Curve around to the left, then enter forested Santa Paula Canyon along the creek. Cross to the north side of the creek, and head up canyon to a fire road at 1.2 miles. Continue up the fire road. Recross the creek at two miles, and begin switchbacking up the mountain. The trail levels off before dropping down into Big Cone Camp on a terrace above Santa Paula Creek. At the far end of the grassy flat, the narrow path descends to Santa Paula Creek in a gorge. Detour to the left, leaving the main trail, and head 30 yards down-stream to a side canyon on the right. A 25-foot waterfall and pool are twenty yards up this canyon. Large boulders lining the pool are perfect for sitting and viewing the falls. This is a good turnaround spot for a 6-mile hike.

To continue, return to the main trail. Cross to the north side of the East Fork Santa Paula Creek, and climb up to a junction. The right fork parallels the East Fork on an unmaintained trail to Cienega Camp and Santa Paula Peak. Take the left fork and head north up Santa Paula Canyon on the Last Chance Trail. Pass the top of the waterfall and a series of pools, falls, and water chutes for a half mile to spruce-shaded Cross Camp. This is our turnaround spot.

To hike further, the trail continues up canyon for miles to the Topatopa Ridge and Hines Peak.

CROSS CAMP

The Punchbowl

LAST CHANCE TRL.

East Fork

SANTA PAULA CANYON

▲ BIG CONE CAMP

ECHO FALLS CANYON

N
E
S
W

Santa Paula Creek

FERNDALE RANCH

THOMAS AQUINAS COLLEGE

150

P

ALSO SEE MAP ON PAGE 22

SANTA PAULA CANYON

Sespe Cr.

TO OJAI

TO SANTA PAULA

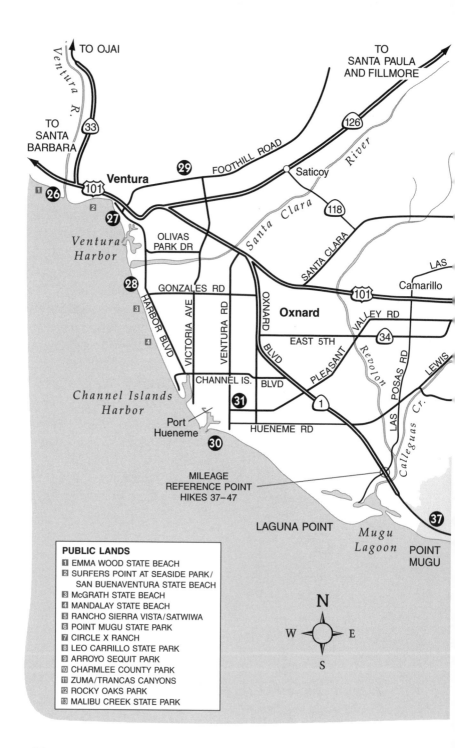

PUBLIC LANDS
1. EMMA WOOD STATE BEACH
2. SURFERS POINT AT SEASIDE PARK/ SAN BUENAVENTURA STATE BEACH
3. McGRATH STATE BEACH
4. MANDALAY STATE BEACH
5. RANCHO SIERRA VISTA/SATWIWA
6. POINT MUGU STATE PARK
7. CIRCLE X RANCH
8. LEO CARRILLO STATE PARK
9. ARROYO SEQUIT PARK
10. CHARMLEE COUNTY PARK
11. ZUMA/TRANCAS CANYONS
12. ROCKY OAKS PARK
13. MALIBU CREEK STATE PARK

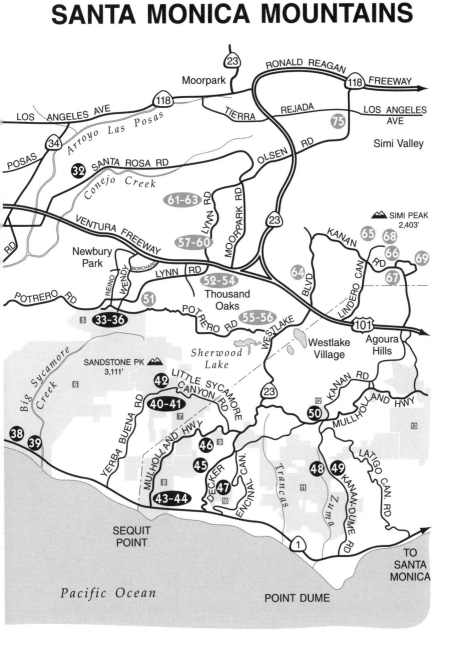

Hike 26
Ocean's Edge—River's Edge Loop
EMMA WOOD STATE BEACH • SEASIDE WILDERNESS PARK

Hiking distance: 2 mile loop
Hiking time: 1 hour
Elevation gain: Level
Maps: U.S.G.S. Ventura
      Emma Wood State Beach map

map
next page

Summary of hike: Emma Wood State Beach, located minutes from the city of Ventura, encompasses 152 acres near the mouth of the Ventura River. The state beach includes a campground, sand and cobblestone beaches, tidepools, sand dunes, a freshwater marsh, and thick riparian foliage. At the mouth of the river is an estuary where the freshwater from the river mixes with the salt water of the sea. Seaside Wilderness Park, adjacent to Emma Wood State Beach, is an undeveloped 22-acre park with a quarter mile of ocean frontage. The Ocean's Edge Trail begins in Emma Wood State Beach and follows the coastline past tidepools into the estuary and surrounding wetlands of Seaside Wilderness Park. The loop hike returns along the Ventura River on the River's Edge Trail.

Driving directions: Driving northbound on Highway 101 (Ventura Freeway) in Ventura, take the California Street exit. Drive a few blocks north to Main Street. Turn left and drive 1.2 miles through downtown Ventura to the Emma Wood State Beach entrance, just before reaching the northbound Highway 101 on-ramp. Turn left and drive 0.4 miles to the far end of the parking lot. A parking fee is required.

    Driving southbound on Highway 101 (Ventura Freeway), take the Main Street/Ventura exit. At the end of the off-ramp, turn right and quickly turn right again into the posted Emma Wood State Beach.

Hiking directions: Take the paved walking path towards the railroad tracks and ocean. Cross through a tunnel under the tracks. Follow the natural path through the chaparral to the rocky oceanfront. Bear left on the Ocean's Edge Trail and stroll the coastline south. Cross a sandy stretch by the Second Mouth estuary, a former outlet of the Ventura River. Walk past the estuary and climb the low dunes to a network of connecting trails in Seaside Wilderness Park at the Ventura River. Bear left on the River's Edge Trail through riparian vegetation and groves of Monterey pines and palms. Parallel the north banks of the river in the Lower Ventura River Estuary. Cross over the railroad tracks, heading upstream to a bench overlooking a bend in the river. Curve away from the river on the wide path, weaving through a tunnel of trees. Cross the grassy picnic area, completing the loop at the parking lot.

Hike 27
San Buenaventura State Beach
to the Ventura River Estuary

Hiking distance: 4 miles round trip
Hiking time: 2 hours
Elevation gain: Level
Maps: U.S.G.S. Ventura

map
next page

Summary of hike: San Buenaventura State Beach is an oceanfront park extending two miles along Pierpont Bay. This hike begins at the park headquarters and follows the coastline west on a paved walking and biking path. The trail passes through Promenade Park (a grassy park at the edge of the beach), Surfers Point at Seaside Park (a popular surfing spot at the south end of Figueroa Street), and Ventura County Fairgrounds Beach (a rock and cobble beach). The hike ends at a wetland estuary where the Ventura River joins the ocean.

Driving directions: From Highway 101 (Ventura Freeway) in Ventura, exit on Seaward Avenue and head west to Harbor Boulevard. Turn right and drive 0.4 miles to San Pedro Street. Turn left and go 0.2 miles to the San Buenaventura State Beach parking lot on the right. A parking fee is required.

Hiking directions: Walk towards the ocean and the sand dunes. Take the paved walking and biking path to the right, heading northbound parallel to the dunes. At a half mile, the path closely parallels Harbor Boulevard. Cross a bridge over a lagoon formed by the San Jon Barranca drainage, reaching the Ventura Pier at just over a mile. For a short detour, walk up the steps and stroll 1,700 feet out to sea on the wooden pier. Continue west of the pier through landscaped Promenade Park, fronted by a wide, sandy beach. The sand soon gives way to the rocky shoreline at Surfers Point at Seaside Park and Ventura County Fairgrounds Beach, lined with palms. At the west end of the pathway, the trail turns inland along the Ventura River and estuary. Across the river is Seaside Wilderness Park and Emma Wood State Beach (Hike 26). This is our turnaround point.

To extend the hike, the Ventura River Trail crosses under Highway 101 and jogs through Ventura to a paved path. The trail continues to Foster Park off of Highway 33, where it becomes the Ojai Valley Trail. It continues 9.5 miles uphill on the old Southern Pacific Railroad to Libbey Park in downtown Ojai.

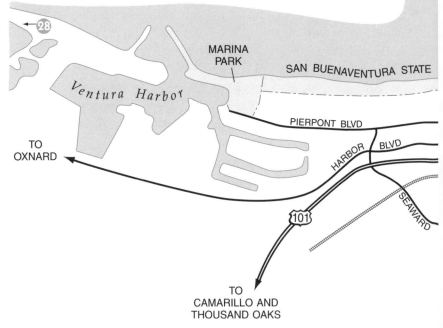

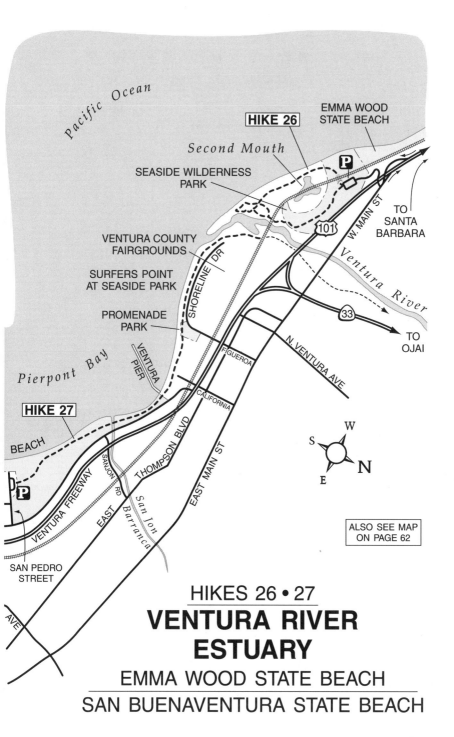

Pacific Ocean

HIKE 26

EMMA WOOD
STATE BEACH

Second Mouth

SEASIDE WILDERNESS
PARK

P

101

W. MAIN ST

TO
SANTA
BARBARA

VENTURA COUNTY
FAIRGROUNDS

SHORELINE DR

Ventura River

SURFERS POINT
AT SEASIDE PARK

33

TO
OJAI

PROMENADE
PARK

Pierpont Bay

VENTURA PIER

FIGUEROA

N. VENTURA AVE

HIKE 27

CALIFORNIA

W

S

N

BEACH

VENTURA FREEWAY

SANJON RD

THOMPSON BLVD

San Jon Barranca

EAST MAIN ST

EAST

E

P

ALSO SEE MAP
ON PAGE 62

SAN PEDRO
STREET

AVE

HIKES 26 • 27
VENTURA RIVER
ESTUARY
EMMA WOOD STATE BEACH
SAN BUENAVENTURA STATE BEACH

Hike 28
Santa Clara Estuary Natural Preserve
McGRATH STATE BEACH

Hiking distance: 0.7 mile loop to 4 miles round trip
Hiking time: 45 minutes—2 hours
Elevation gain: Level
Maps: U.S.G.S. Oxnard
    McGrath State Beach map

Summary of hike: McGrath State Beach is located on the west end of Oxnard just south of Ventura. Rolling sand dunes, stabilized with vegetation, line the two-mile long coastline of this 295-acre park. The northern 160 acres comprise the Santa Clara Estuary Natural Preserve, where fresh water from the Santa Clara River mixes with the ocean's salt water. The Santa Clara Nature Trail follows the south banks of the river through the estuary and wildlife refuge, crossing low dunes to the ocean. McGrath Lake, a small freshwater lake at the southern end of McGrath State Beach, attracts hundreds of bird species.

Driving directions: From Highway 101 (Ventura Freeway) in Ventura, take the Victoria Avenue exit, and drive 0.6 miles south to Olivas Park Drive. Turn right and drive 2.4 miles to Harbor Boulevard. Turn left and continue 1.1 mile to the posted McGrath State Beach entrance at 2211 Harbor Boulevard. Turn right and go 0.2 miles to the trailhead parking lot, just beyond the entrance station. A parking fee is required.

Hiking directions: Walk to the far (north) end of the parking lot and curve right. Cross a wooden footbridge and enter a riparian habitat of sandbar willow thickets, cottonwoods, coastal scrub, and freshwater marsh plants. A raised boardwalk winds through the fragile wetlands to the banks of the Santa Clara River. Return 30 yards and continue on the path downstream to a levee. A path to the left returns to the parking area for a half-mile loop. Continue along the river and climb over the sand dunes to the mouth of the river at the ocean. This is a good turnaround spot for a shorter walk.

To extend the hike, follow the sandy coastline one mile south to the north end of McGrath Lake, peacefully hidden in the dunes. To spot it, walk to the top reaches of the beach, and drop down to the lake. Beyond the lake's south shore, the sandy coastline continues along Mandalay County Beach.

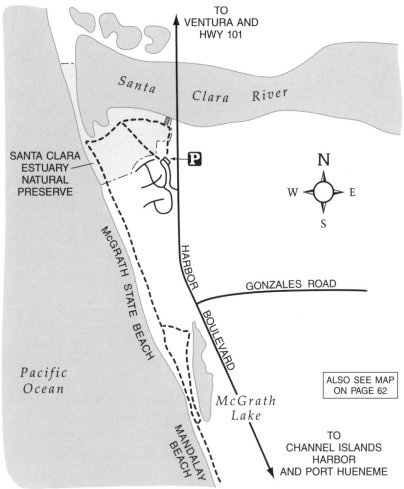

SANTA CLARA ESTUARY
NATURAL PRESERVE
McGRATH STATE BEACH

Hike 29
Arroyo Verde Park

Hiking distance: 3 mile loop
Hiking time: 1.5 hours
Elevation gain: 200 feet
Maps: U.S.G.S. Saticoy

Summary of hike: Arroyo Verde Park is a 129-acre park in the city of Ventura. The park sits in a small canyon between Barlow Canyon to the west and Sexton Canyon to the east. On the south end of the park is a developed 14-acre open grassy area. To the north is a natural, chaparral covered canyon area. A series of trails lead up the hillsides to excellent views above the developed portion of the park.

Driving directions: From Highway 101 (Ventura Freeway) in Ventura, exit on Victoria Avenue. Head 2.2 miles north to the end of Victoria Avenue at Foothill Road. Turn left and continue 0.7 miles to Arroyo Verde Park, opposite of Day Road. Turn right into the park entrance. Park past the nature center in the first lot.

Hiking directions: The trail begins near the park entrance across the lawn from the Arroyo Verde Center. You may also pick up the trail by crossing the lawn to the west from the parking lot. The trail heads north, traversing the hillside along the forested route. At 0.8 miles, the trail descends at Vista Bluff and meets the park road by Redwood Glen. Cross the road, picking up the backcountry trail, and continue north into the canyon. A short distance ahead is a junction. The left fork, the higher route, loops around the hillside and rejoins the right fork at the north end of the canyon below The Wall, a 600-foot vertical mountain boxing in the head of the canyon. From the end of the canyon, head to the right (southeast) 50 yards to another junction. The left fork heads up the hillside, returning along the eastern side of the park. The right fork follows the canyon floor, returning along the most direct route.

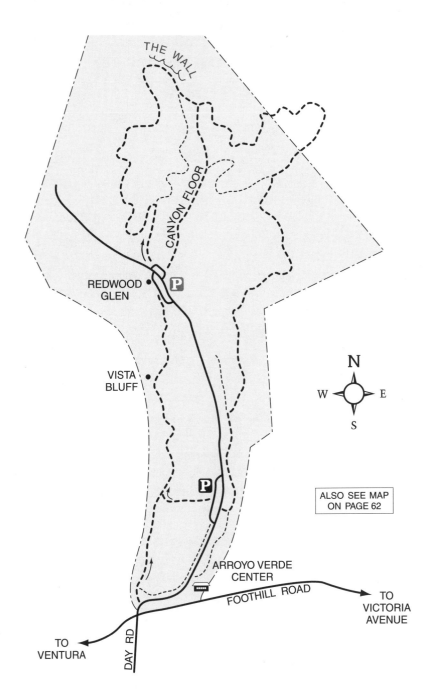

THE WALL

CANYON FLOOR

REDWOOD
GLEN

P

VISTA
BLUFF

P

N
W ⊕ E
S

ALSO SEE MAP
ON PAGE 62

ARROYO VERDE
CENTER

FOOTHILL ROAD

TO
VICTORIA
AVENUE

DAY RD

TO
VENTURA

ARROYO VERDE PARK

Hike 30
Port Hueneme Beach Park

Hiking distance: 2.5 miles round trip
Hiking time: 1.5 hours
Elevation gain: Level
Maps: U.S.G.S. Oxnard

Summary of hike: Port Hueneme Beach Park is a landscaped and well-maintained park to the southeast of the 1,600-acre Port Hueneme Naval Construction Battalion Center. The 50-acre park has a wide sandy beach and a wooden, T-shaped recreational pier that extends 1,240 feet out to sea. From the pier are great views of the Ventura County coastline, the Channel Islands, and the Santa Monica Mountains at Point Mugu. A path runs along the edge of the beach, ending at the harbor entrance of the naval complex.

Driving directions: Heading northbound on Highway 101 (Ventura Freeway) in Oxnard, take the Ventura Road exit, and drive 7 miles south to Surfside Drive at the beachfront. Turn left and drive 0.2 miles to the beach parking lot on the right. A parking fee is required.

Heading southbound on Highway 101 (Ventura Freeway) in Oxnard, take the Wagon Wheel Road exit, and turn right a half block to Ventura Road. Turn left and drive 7 miles south to Surfside Drive at the beachfront.

Hiking directions: Take the paved, palm-lined path curving south and looping by Bubbling Springs (Hike 31). Heading southeast away from the walkway is Ormand Beach, an undeveloped natural area with low rolling sand dunes and a wide sandy beach that extends 3 miles along the coast. Port Hueneme Beach Park lies west towards Port Hueneme Pier. Stroll out on the pier, and take in the sweeping vistas from offshore. Continue west from the pier, either beachcombing or following the walking path to the west end of Surfside Drive. Beyond the walkway, a wide gravel path follows the shoreline to the mouth of Port

Hueneme Harbor, between the oceanfront jetty boulders and the shipping docks. At the harbor channel is the Port Hueneme Lighthouse, originally built in 1874 and rebuilt in 1941. Return by retracing your steps.

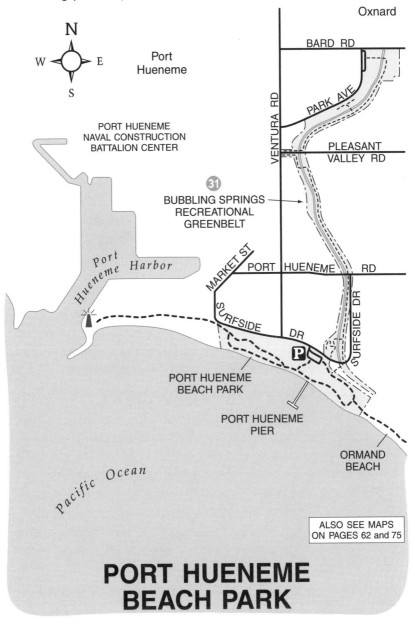

ALSO SEE MAPS
ON PAGES 62 and 75

PORT HUENEME
BEACH PARK

Hike 31
Bubbling Springs Recreational Greenbelt

Hiking distance: 3.6 miles round trip
Hiking time: 2 hours
Elevation gain: Level
Maps: U.S.G.S. Oxnard
The Thomas Guide—Ventura County

Summary of hike: Bubbling Springs Park is a long, narrow greenbelt extending from Port Hueneme's inner residential area to the ocean at Port Hueneme Beach Park. A 1.5-mile hiking and biking path winds through the landscaped recreational corridor alongside tranquil Bubbling Springs, a tree-shaded drainage channel.

Driving directions: From Highway 101 (Ventura Freeway) in Oxnard, take the Ventura Road exit, and drive 6 miles south to Bard Road. Turn left and drive 0.3 miles to Bubbling Springs Park. Turn right on Park Avenue and park in the spaces on the left.

Heading southbound on Highway 101 (Ventura Freeway) in Oxnard, take the Wagon Wheel Road exit, and turn right a half block to Ventura Road. Turn left and drive 6 miles south to Bard Road. Turn left and drive 0.3 miles to Bubbling Springs Park. Turn right on Park Avenue and park in the spaces on the left.

Hiking directions: Cross the grassy park by the ball fields to the paved hiking and biking path on the east edge of the greenbelt. Take the path to the right, and head south alongside Bubbling Springs, lined with eucalyptus trees. At 0.3 miles is a bridge crossing over the stream to an open parkland. The path stays on the east side of the waterway, passing the community center to Pleasant Valley Road at 0.6 miles. Cross the intersection at Ventura Road, and continue on the signed walking path. Curve left, crossing a bridge over the creek, and follow the tree-lined watercourse downstream, reaching Port Hueneme Road at 1.1 mile. Cross the boulevard and continue south, parallel to the creek and Surfside Drive. Another bridge crosses the creek to an expansive grassy section of Bubbling Springs Linear Park and its baseball fields. The streamside trail meanders through palm tree groves to Surfside Drive. Cross the road to Port Hueneme Beach Park, where the trail ends. To extend the hike along the coastline, continue with Hike 30.

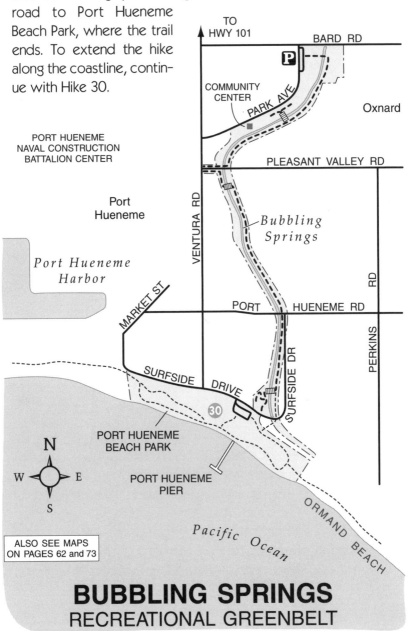

BUBBLING SPRINGS
RECREATIONAL GREENBELT

Hike 32
Mission Oaks Community Park Trail

Hiking distance: 2 miles round trip
Hiking time: 1 hour
Elevation gain: 100 feet
Maps: U.S.G.S. Camarillo

Summary of hike: The Mission Oaks Park Trail leads through a natural area with hills and canyons connecting Mission Oaks Park and Mission Verde Park. Mission Oaks Park is a developed park with baseball fields, tennis courts, and a picnic area. Mission Verde Park is a grassy hilltop flat overlooking the open space. The forested trail parallels a seasonal waterway.

Driving directions: From Highway 101 (Ventura Freeway) in Camarillo, take the Pleasant Valley Road/Santa Rosa Road exit. Drive 1.6 miles north to Oak Canyon Road and turn left. Continue 0.4 miles—crossing Mission Oaks Boulevard—to Mission Oaks Community Park. Park in the lot to the left near the tennis courts.

Hiking directions: From the parking lot, walk between the tennis courts and Mission Oaks Boulevard to the trailhead. The path leads downhill and crosses a wooden footbridge to a five-way junction. Continue straight ahead on the main path. After crossing a drainage creek, the trail curves to the right. Take the narrow side path on the left that leads up the hill into Mission Verde Park. Return to the main trail, and continue north to a trail split. Take the left fork up the draw. Near the northwest corner of the park, the trail heads up a short hill to a junction. The left fork leads to Woodcreek Road. Take the right fork east across the head of the canyon. Descend back down into the canyon, completing the loop. Retrace your steps to the five-way junction. Take the right fork through the tunnel under the road. The trail curves 0.4 miles through a wooded area and ends at Santa Rosa Road. Return along the same path.

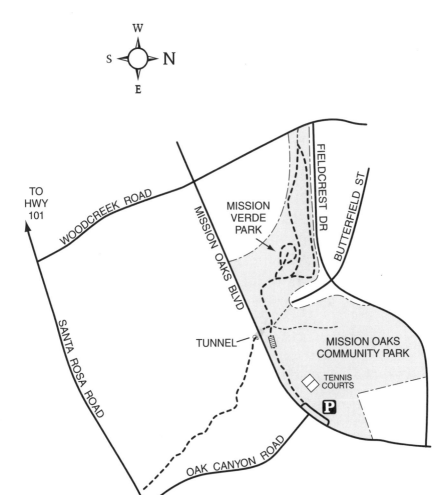

TO HWY 101

WOODCREEK ROAD

SANTA ROSA ROAD

MISSION OAKS BLVD

MISSION VERDE PARK

FIELDCREST DR

BUTTERFIELD ST

TUNNEL

MISSION OAKS COMMUNITY PARK

TENNIS COURTS

P

OAK CANYON ROAD

ALSO SEE MAP ON PAGE 62

MISSION OAKS
COMMUNITY PARK TRAIL

Hike 33
Ranch Overlook Trail—Satwiwa Loop
RANCHO SIERRA VISTA/SATWIWA

Hiking distance: 2.5 mile loop
Hiking time: 1.5 hours
Elevation gain: 300 feet
Maps: U.S.G.S. Newbury Park
      Santa Monica Mountains West Trail Map
      N.P.S. Rancho Sierra Vista/Satwiwa map

map
next page

Summary of hike: Rancho Sierra Vista/Satwiwa is located at the south edge of Newbury Park and on the northern boundary of Point Mugu State Park. The historical site is named for its two cultural legacies. For thousands of years it was the ancestral land of the Chumash and Gabrielino Indians. It was also a horse and cattle ranch named Rancho Sierra Vista. In 1980, an area of the parkland, part of the Santa Monica Mountains National Recreation Area, was designated as the Native American Indian Cultural Center and Natural Area. The site hosts a network of hiking trails. This hike loops through the rolling grasslands and chaparral to the hills that surround the meadow.

Driving directions: From Highway 101 (Ventura Freeway) in Newbury Park, exit on Wendy Drive. Drive 2 miles south to Lynn Road. Turn right and continue 1.7 miles to Via Goleta, the park entrance road. Turn left and drive 0.7 miles to the main parking lot at the end of the road.

Hiking directions: Walk back up the entrance road 0.1 mile to the posted Ranch Overlook Trail on the left. Bear left and climb the hill overlooking Rancho Sierra Vista, the Satwiwa Natural Area, the jagged Boney Mountain ridge, and Big Sycamore Canyon. Follow the ridge east to a junction with the main park road. To the right is the head of Big Sycamore Canyon (Hike 36), and left leads to Potrero Road. Cross the road over two bridges to the cultural center on the left and a Chumash demonstration village on the right. Take the signed Satwiwa

Loop Trail, passing an old cattle pond on the right. Cross the grasslands toward the windmill, which can be seen on the hillside ahead. As you near the windmill, drop into an oak-shaded ravine and cross a seasonal stream. Climb a short distance to the windmill and a junction. Bear to the right and traverse the upper slope of the meadow to a Y-fork. Stay to the left on the Hidden Valley Connector Trail. Head 50 yards to a magnificent overlook of Hidden Valley and Big Sycamore Canyon. Go to the right and follow the ridge downhill to a trail split. The left fork leads to a waterfall (Hike 35). Continue straight to a 3-way trail split at the top of the meadow. Take the middle fork, completing the loop at the cultural center. Cross the road and return to the parking area on the wide gravel path.

Hike 34
Wendy—Satwiwa Loop Trail
RANCHO SIERRA VISTA/SATWIWA

Hiking distance: 2.2 mile loop
Hiking time: 1 hour
Elevation gain: 200 feet
Maps: U.S.G.S. Newbury Park

map
next page

Santa Monica Mountains West Trail Map
N.P.S. Rancho Sierra Vista/Satwiwa map

Summary of hike: Rancho Sierra Vista/Satwiwa sits on the bluffs at the head of Big Sycamore Canyon on the northern boundary of Point Mugu State Park. The Satwiwa Native American Indian Natural Area was occupied for thousands of years by the Chumash and Gabrielino Indians. Satwiwa, the name of the Chumash village, means "the bluffs." This hike explores the open rolling terrain covered with chaparral and grasslands and the forested ravines with oaks and sycamores. The prominent volcanic cliffs of Boney Mountain are in view throughout the hike.

Driving directions: From Highway 101 (Ventura Freeway) in Newbury Park, exit on Wendy Drive. Drive 2.7 miles south to

Potrero Road. Park in the parking area straight ahead, across the road.

Hiking directions: Head southwest past a signed junction with the Los Robles Connector Trail, and cross the grassy slopes dotted with oaks and sycamores. At 0.3 miles is a signed junction, the start of the loop. Leave the Wendy Trail for now, and bear left towards the windmill. Climb a short, steep hill to another junction. Again bear left, reaching the windmill and a junction at a half mile. Both trail forks follow the Satwiwa Loop Trail. The left fork leads to the Boney Mountain Trail. Take the right fork, and descend through a narrow ravine under an oak-shaded canopy. Cross the drainage and follow the open slopes, passing an unsigned path. Curve around the hillside to a 4-way junction by a pond. Straight ahead is the cultural center. The left fork leads to the pond. Bear right and climb to a junction at the crest of the hill. Take the right fork, staying on the Wendy Trail. Traverse the hillside northeast and complete the loop. Return to the left.

S

E ← ⬥ → W

N

HIKES 33 • 34
RANCHO
SIERRA VISTA/SATWIWA
RANCH OVERLOOK–SATWIWA LOOP
WENDY–SATWIWA LOOP

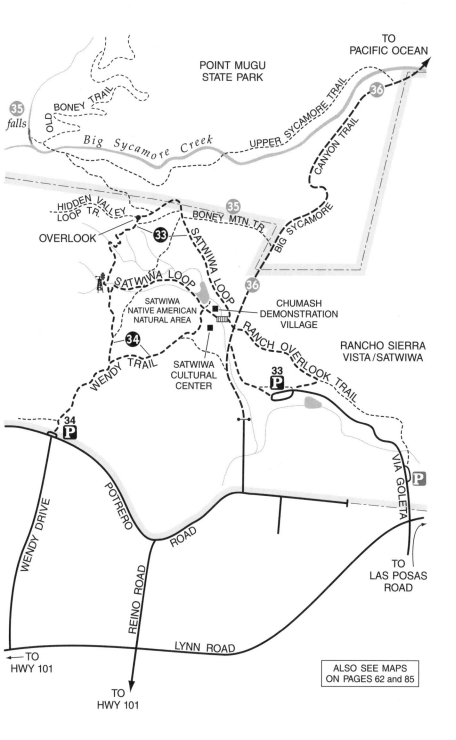

POINT MUGU
STATE PARK

TO
PACIFIC OCEAN

UPPER SYCAMORE TRAIL

CANYON TRAIL

35
falls

OLD BONEY TRAIL

Big Sycamore Creek

HIDDEN VALLEY
LOOP TR.

BONEY MTN. TR. **35**

OVERLOOK

33

SATWIWA LOOP

BIG SYCAMORE

SATWIWA LOOP

36

SATWIWA
NATIVE AMERICAN
NATURAL AREA

CHUMASH
DEMONSTRATION
VILLAGE

RANCHO SIERRA
VISTA/SATWIWA

34

WENDY TRAIL

SATWIWA
CULTURAL
CENTER

RANCH OVERLOOK TRAIL

33
P

34
P

VIA GOLETA

P

WENDY DRIVE

POTRERO

ROAD

REINO ROAD

TO
LAS POSAS
ROAD

LYNN ROAD

← TO
HWY 101

TO
HWY 101

ALSO SEE MAPS
ON PAGES 62 and 85

Hike 35
Boney Mountain Trail
to Sycamore Canyon Falls

RANCHO SIERRA VISTA/SATWIWA
POINT MUGU STATE PARK

Hiking distance: 3 miles round trip
Hiking time: 1.5 hours
Elevation gain: 350 feet
Maps: U.S.G.S. Newbury Park
       Santa Monica Mountains West Trail Map
       N.P.S. Rancho Sierra Vista/Satwiwa map

Summary of hike: The Boney Mountain Trail climbs up the west slope of Boney Mountain at the upper reaches of Point Mugu State Park. This hike leads to a layered waterfall, locally known as Sycamore Canyon Falls. The waterfall is surrounded by deep sandstone walls, lush vegetation, and small pools in the shade of a dense sycamore, bay, and oak forest. The hike begins in the Rancho Sierra Vista/Satwiwa area, an early ranching site and former Native American Indian land.

Driving directions: From Highway 101 (Ventura Freeway) in Newbury Park, exit on Wendy Drive. Drive 2 miles south to Lynn Road. Turn right and continue 1.7 miles to Via Goleta, the park entrance road. Turn left and drive 0.7 miles to the main parking lot at the end of the road.

Hiking directions: Take the posted trail past the restrooms a quarter mile to the service road at the Satwiwa Native American Indian Cultural Center. Bear right on the road, entering Point Mugu State Park. As you approach the ridge overlooking Big Sycamore Canyon, take the Boney Mountain Trail to the left along the brink of the canyon. Climb a short hill, passing the Satwiwa Loop Trail on the left, and continue around a ridge to a trail split. Take the right fork, descending down to the forested canyon floor. Stay on the main trail, and cross the streambed where the trail switchbacks sharply to the right. Instead of taking this horseshoe turn to the right, bear to the left, taking the footpath 100 yards to a stream crossing and the waterfall. After enjoying the falls, return along the same trail.

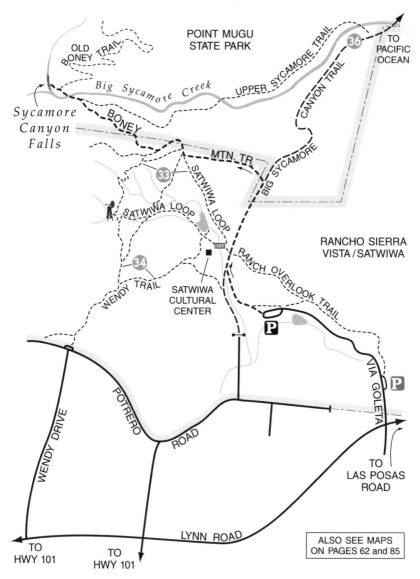

BONEY MOUNTAIN TRAIL
TO SYCAMORE CANYON FALLS

Hike 36
Big Sycamore Canyon Trail
POINT MUGU STATE PARK

Hiking distance: 8.4 miles one way (car shuttle)
Hiking time: 3 hours
Elevation loss: 900 feet
Maps: U.S.G.S. Newbury Park, Camarillo, and Point Mugu
Santa Monica Mountains West Trail Map
N.P.S. Rancho Sierra Vista/Satwiwa map

Summary of hike: The Big Sycamore Canyon Trail is a one-way mountains-to-the-sea journey. The trail, an unpaved service road, connects Newbury Park with the Sycamore Canyon Campground at the Pacific Ocean. The hike parallels Big Sycamore Creek through the heart of Point Mugu State Park in a deep, wooded canyon under towering sycamores and oaks.

Driving directions: For the shuttle car, follow the driving directions to Hike 39 and leave the car in the parking lot, where this hike ends.

To the trailhead: From the shuttle car parking lot, drive 5.8 miles northbound on the Pacific Coast Highway (Highway 1) to Las Posas Road. Take Las Posas Road 2.9 miles north to Hueneme Road—turn right. Continue one mile to West Potrero Road and turn right. Drive 5.4 miles to Via Goleta and turn right (En route, West Potrero Road becomes Lynn Road). Drive 0.7 miles on Via Goleta to the parking lot at the end of the road.

Hiking directions: Take the posted trail past the restrooms a quarter mile to the service road at the Satwiwa Native American Indian Cultural Center. Bear right on the road, entering Point Mugu State Park, to a junction with the Boney Mountain Trail on the left (Hike 35). Begin the winding descent on the paved road to the canyon floor. The trail crosses a wooden bridge over the creek to the Hidden Pond Trail junction on the right. This is an excellent single track alternative trail that rejoins the Big Sycamore Canyon Trail 1.7 miles down canyon. On the alternative trail, there is a split at 2.2 miles. Take the left fork to the Sycamore Camping and Picnic Area. At 3 miles is a signed "beach" path on the right. This is where the alternative trail rejoins the service road. Just past the junction is the Danielson Ranch. Past the ranch, the trail is unpaved. Continue south down the forested canyon, past the Backbone Trail and the Overlook Trail (Hike 39) to the gate. From the gate, a paved road leads back to the shuttle car.

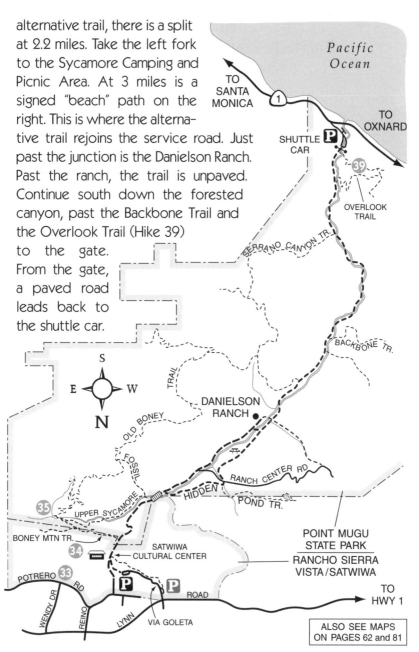

ALSO SEE MAPS ON PAGES 62 and 81

BIG SYCAMORE CANYON
POINT MUGU STATE PARK

Hike 37
Chumash Trail—Mugu Peak Loop
POINT MUGU STATE PARK

Hiking distance: 4.5 mile loop
Hiking time: 2.5 hours
Elevation gain: 1,100 feet
Maps: U.S.G.S. Point Mugu
Santa Monica Mountains West Trail Map

*map
next page*

Summary of hike: La Jolla Valley Natural Preserve is an expansive high-mountain valley at the far western end of the Santa Monica Mountains. The oak-studded grassland rests 800 feet above the ocean at the foot of Mugu Peak in Point Mugu State Park. The high ridges of Laguna Peak, La Jolla Peak, and the serrated Boney Mountain ridgeline surround the rolling meadow. La Jolla Valley can be accessed from La Jolla Canyon (Hike 38), Big Sycamore Canyon (Hike 36), and the Chumash Trail (this hike), the steepest and most direct route. For centuries, this trail was a Chumash Indian route connecting their coastal village at Mugu Lagoon with La Jolla Valley. This hike steeply ascends the coastal slope on the west flank of Mugu Peak. The elevated Mugu Peak Trail circles the mountain slope below the double peak, with sweeping ocean and mountain vistas.

Driving directions: From the Pacific Coast Highway (Highway 1) and Las Posas Road in southeast Oxnard, drive 2.3 miles southbound on PCH to the large parking pullout on the left, across from the Navy Rifle Range and Mugu Lagoon.
    Heading northbound on the Pacific Coast Highway, the trailhead parking area is 16.8 miles past Malibu/Kanan Dume Road and 3.5 miles west of the well-marked Sycamore Canyon.

Hiking directions: Begin climbing up the chaparral and cactus covered hillside, gaining elevation with every step. At a half mile, the trail temporarily levels out on a plateau with sweeping coastal views, including the Channel Islands. The steadily ascending trail gains 900 feet in 0.7 miles to a T-junction on a saddle. Begin the loop to the left, crossing over the saddle into the vast La Jolla Valley. The valley is surrounded by rounded mountain peaks, the jagged Boney Mountain ridge, and the surrealistic Navy radar towers by Laguna Peak. Cross the open expanse to a posted junction with the La Jolla Valley Loop Trail at 1.2 miles. Take the right fork and head southeast across the meadow on a slight downward slope. Drop into an oak woodland and cross a stream. Parallel the stream through a small draw to a another junction. Take the right fork 100 yards to a path on the right by an old metal tank. Bear right on the Mugu Peak Trail, and cross the creek. Traverse the hillside to the west edge of La Jolla Canyon. Follow the ridge south on the oceanfront cliffs. Wind along the south flank of Mugu Peak, following the contours of the mountain to a trail split on a saddle between the mountain's double peaks. The right fork ascends the rounded grassy summit. Veer left, hiking along the steep hillside to the west side of the peak. Cross another saddle and complete the loop. Return down the mountain to the trailhead.

Hike 38
La Jolla Valley Loop from La Jolla Canyon
POINT MUGU STATE PARK

Hiking distance: 6 miles round trip
Hiking time: 3 hours
Elevation gain: 750 feet
Maps: U.S.G.S. Point Mugu
      Santa Monica Mountains West Trail Map

**map
next page**

Summary of hike: La Jolla Canyon is a narrow, steep gorge with a perennial stream and a 15-foot waterfall. The canyon leads up to La Jolla Valley Natural Preserve at an 800-foot elevation, a broad valley with rolling grasslands at the west end of the Santa Monica Mountains. Mugu Peak, La Jolla Peak, and Laguna Peak surround the oak-dotted meadow. This hike climbs through the rock-walled canyon and loops around the meadow to a coastal overlook and a pond with a picnic area.

Driving directions: From the Pacific Coast Highway (Highway 1) and Las Posas Road in southeast Oxnard, drive 4.2 miles southbound on PCH to the posted La Jolla Canyon entrance on the left.

Heading northbound on the Pacific Coast Highway, the trailhead parking area is 15 miles past Malibu/Kanan Dume Road and 1.6 miles west of the well-marked Sycamore Canyon.

Hiking directions: From the north end of the parking lot, at the Ray Miller Trailhead, take the La Jolla Canyon Trail north. Follow the wide path up the canyon, crossing the stream several times. The third crossing is just below a beautiful 15-foot waterfall and a pool surrounded by large boulders. Natural rock steps lead up to the top of the falls. The trail continues along the east side of the canyon, passing large sandstone rocks and caves. At a gorge, the trail sharply doubles back to the right, leading up the side of the canyon. At 1.2 miles, take the left fork towards Mugu Peak. Cross the stream and head southwest to a ridge above La Jolla Canyon and the ocean. The trail levels out and passes two trail junctions. Stay to the right both times, heading north across the rolling grassland. At 2.7 miles the trail joins the wide La Jolla Valley Loop Trail—head to the right. As you near the mountains of La Jolla Canyon, take the first cutoff trail to the right, leading past the pond and rejoining the La Jolla Canyon Trail. Head to the right, and go two miles down canyon, returning to the trailhead.

TO OXNARD

Mugu Lagoon

HIKES 37–38
LA JOLLA VALLEY
MUGU PEAK
POINT MUGU STATE PARK

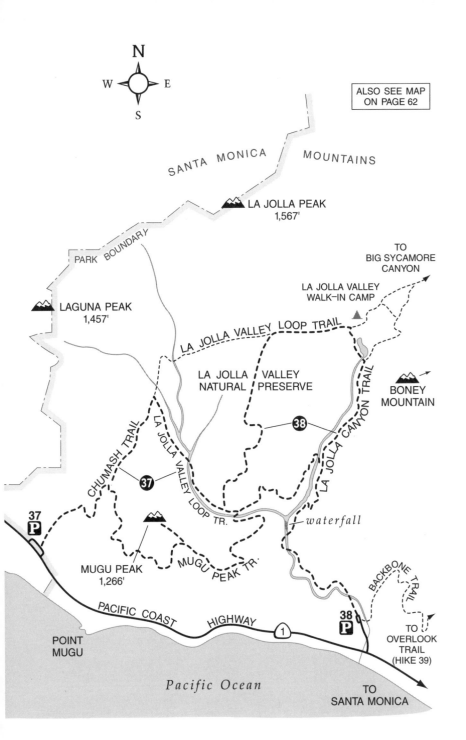

N
W E
S

ALSO SEE MAP
ON PAGE 62

SANTA MONICA MOUNTAINS

LA JOLLA PEAK
1,567'

PARK BOUNDARY

TO
BIG SYCAMORE
CANYON

LA JOLLA VALLEY
WALK-IN CAMP

LAGUNA PEAK
1,457'

LA JOLLA VALLEY LOOP TRAIL

LA JOLLA VALLEY
NATURAL PRESERVE

BONEY
MOUNTAIN

38

LA JOLLA CANYON TRAIL

CHUMASH TRAIL

LA JOLLA VALLEY LOOP TR.

37

37
P

waterfall

MUGU PEAK
1,266'

MUGU PEAK TR.

BACKBONE TRAIL

PACIFIC COAST HIGHWAY

1

38
P

TO
OVERLOOK
TRAIL
(HIKE 39)

POINT
MUGU

Pacific Ocean

TO
SANTA MONICA

Hike 39
Scenic and Overlook Trails Loop
POINT MUGU STATE PARK

Hiking distance: 2 mile loop
Hiking time: 1 hour
Elevation gain: 900 feet
Maps: U.S.G.S. Point Mugu
　　　　Santa Monica Mountains West Trail Map

Summary of hike: The Scenic and Overlook Trails are located along the coastal frontage of Point Mugu State Park. The trail follows the ridge separating Big Sycamore Canyon from La Jolla Canyon. This short but beautiful hike climbs up the chaparral covered ridge to several panoramic overlooks of the Pacific Ocean.

Driving directions: From the Pacific Coast Highway (Highway 1) and Las Posas Road in southeast Oxnard, drive 5.8 miles southbound on PCH to the posted Big Sycamore Canyon entrance on the left. Turn left and park in the day-use pay parking lot 0.1 mile ahead on the left. Parking is free in pullouts along PCH.

Heading northbound on the Pacific Coast Highway, the trailhead parking entrance is on the right, 13.3 miles past Malibu/Kanan Dume Road and 5.3 miles west of the well-marked Leo Carrillo State Beach.

Hiking directions: From the parking area, walk up the road past the campground to the Big Sycamore Canyon trailhead gate. Continue up the unpaved road about 50 yards to the signed junction with the Scenic Trail. Take the trail to the left (west) across Big Sycamore Creek, and head up the wooden steps. The trail steadily gains elevation up an open, grassy hillside with good canyon views. At the saddle near the top of the hill is a trail split. The left fork leads a short distance to an ocean overlook. Continue up to several more viewpoints. Return back to the junction, and head north to a junction with the Overlook Trail. Take this service road downhill to the right, winding 0.9 miles back to the Big Sycamore Canyon floor. Near the bottom, a series of five gentle switchbacks lead to the junction. Take the canyon trail to the right, leading 0.4 miles back to the trailhead gate.

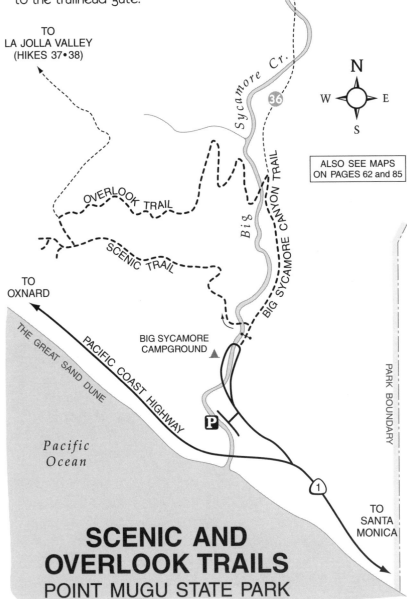

TO
LA JOLLA VALLEY
(HIKES 37•38)

Sycamore Cr.

36

N
W ← → E
S

ALSO SEE MAPS
ON PAGES 62 and 85

OVERLOOK TRAIL

Big BIG SYCAMORE CANYON TRAIL

SCENIC TRAIL

TO
OXNARD

THE GREAT SAND DUNE

PACIFIC COAST HIGHWAY

BIG SYCAMORE
CAMPGROUND

PARK BOUNDARY

*Pacific
Ocean*

P

1

TO
SANTA
MONICA

SCENIC AND
OVERLOOK TRAILS
POINT MUGU STATE PARK

Hike 40
Grotto Trail
CIRCLE X RANCH

Hiking distance: 3.5 miles round trip
Hiking time: 2 hours
Elevation gain: 650 feet
Maps: U.S.G.S. Triunfo Pass
Santa Monica Mountains West Trail Map
N.P.S. Circle X Ranch Site

Summary of hike: The Grotto Trail is located in the 1,655-acre Circle X Ranch bordering Point Mugu State Park. Once a Boy Scout wilderness retreat, the Circle X Ranch is now a national park and recreation area. The Grotto, at the end of this trail, is a maze of large, volcanic boulders in a sheer, narrow gorge formed from landslides. The West Fork of the Arroyo Sequit flows through the caves and caverns of The Grotto, creating cascades and pools.

Driving directions: From the Pacific Coast Highway (Highway 1) and Las Posas Road in southeast Oxnard, drive 9 miles southbound to Yerba Buena Road, located 3.3 miles past Sycamore Canyon. Turn left and drive 5.3 winding miles up Yerba Buena Road to the Circle X Ranger Station on the right. Park by the ranger station, or drive 0.2 miles downhill to the day-use parking area, just past the posted Grotto Trailhead.
Heading northbound on the Pacific Coast Highway from Malibu, Yerba Buena Road is 2 miles past Leo Carrillo State Beach. Turn right and follow the directions above.

Hiking directions: From the ranger station, walk 0.2 miles down the unpaved road to the posted Grotto trailhead, just before reaching the lower parking area. Continue downhill, crossing the West Fork of Arroyo Sequit. At 0.4 miles, the trail passes the Canyon View Trail (Hike 41) and recrosses the creek at a 30-foot waterfall. After crossing, curve left, traversing a grassy ridge. Descend to the canyon floor where the trail joins the Happy Hollow Campground Road at 1.2 miles. Follow the road to the left into a primitive campground and cross the creek, picking up the posted Grotto Trail again. Head downstream to a bridge that crosses the creek into the Happy Hollow Campground. Instead of crossing the bridge, continue straight ahead and cross the creek by a pumphouse. Follow the creek a few hundred feet to The Grotto.

After exploring The Grotto, return to the bridge that accesses the campground. Walk through the campground to the road and bear to the right. Follow the winding road, and rejoin the Grotto Trail on the left. Retrace your steps to the parking lot.

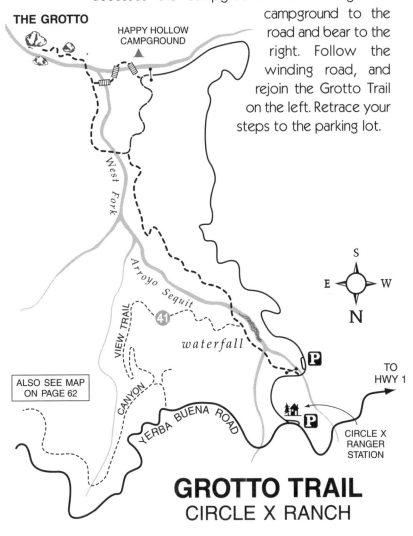

THE GROTTO

HAPPY HOLLOW CAMPGROUND

West Fork

Arroyo Sequit

VIEW TRAIL

41

waterfall

CANYON

ALSO SEE MAP ON PAGE 62

YERBA BUENA ROAD

S
E — W
N

P

TO HWY 1

P

CIRCLE X RANGER STATION

GROTTO TRAIL
CIRCLE X RANCH

Hike 41
Canyon View—
Yerba Buena Road Loop
CIRCLE X RANCH

Hiking distance: 3.2 mile loop
Hiking time: 1.5 hours
Elevation gain: 500 feet
Maps: U.S.G.S. Triunfo Pass
      Santa Monica Mountains West Trail Map
      N.P.S. Circle X Ranch Site

Summary of hike: Circle X Ranch sits below Boney Mountain in the upper canyons of Arroyo Sequit. The Canyon View Trail traverses the brushy hillside of the deep, east-facing canyon. The panoramic views extend down the canyon to the Pacific Ocean. The northern views reach the jagged Boney Mountain ridge and the 3,111-foot Sandstone Peak, the highest peak in the Santa Monica Mountains. The trail connects the Grotto Trail (Hike 40) with the Backbone Trail (Hike 42).

Driving directions: Same as Hike 40.

Hiking directions: From the ranger station, walk 0.2 miles down the unpaved road to the posted Grotto Trailhead, just before reaching the lower parking area. Pass the trail gate and follow the dirt road past a picnic area to another trail sign. Take the footpath downhill and cross the West Fork Arroyo Creek. Parallel the east side of the creek to a signed junction. (Twenty yards to the right is a waterfall—Hike 40.) Bear left on the Canyon View Trail, and traverse the canyon wall, following the contours of the mountain. Climb two switchbacks to a junction. For a shorter 1.5-mile loop, take the Connector Trail 100 yards to the left, reaching Yerba Buena Road, and return 0.35 miles to the ranger station. For this longer hike, stay to the right and cross a rocky wash. Head up the hillside to a south view down canyon to the ocean and the Channel Islands and a north view of the Boney Mountain ridge. Continue to Yerba Buena Road, across from the Backbone Trail (Hike 42). Return to the left on Yerba Buena Road, and walk 1.1 mile back to the trailhead at the Circle X Ranger Station.

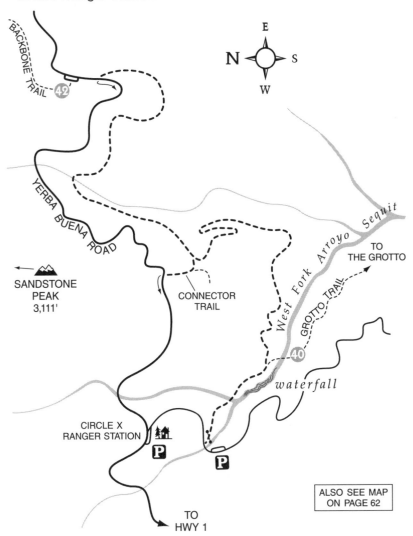

CANYON VIEW TRAIL–
YERBA BUENA ROAD
CIRCLE X RANCH

Hike 42
Sandstone Peak Loop
Mishe Mokwa—Backbone Trails
CIRCLE X RANCH

Hiking distance: 6 mile loop
Hiking time: 3 hours
Elevation gain: 1,100 feet
Maps: U.S.G.S. Triunfo Pass and Newbury Park
Santa Monica Mountains West Trail Map
N.P.S. Circle X Ranch Site

Summary of hike: The Mishe Mokwa Trail in Circle X Ranch follows Carlisle Canyon along Boney Mountain past weathered red volcanic formations. There are views of the sculpted caves and crevices of Echo Cliffs and a forested streamside picnic area by a huge, split boulder known as Split Rock. The return route on the Backbone Trail leads to Inspiration Point and Sandstone Peak, the highest point in the Santa Monica Mountains. Both points overlook the Pacific Ocean, the Channel Islands, and the surrounding mountains.

Driving directions: Follow the directions for Hike 40 to the Circle X Ranger Station. From the ranger station, continue one mile to the Backbone Trailhead parking lot on the left.

Hiking directions: Take the Backbone Trail (a fire road) uphill to the north. At 0.3 miles, leave the road and take the signed Mishe Mokwa Connector Trail straight ahead. Continue 0.2 miles to a junction with the Mishe Mokwa Trail and take the left fork. The trail contours along Boney Mountain on the western edge of Carlisle Canyon. At 1.4 miles, Balanced Rock can be seen on the opposite side of the canyon. Descend into the canyon shaded by laurel, oak, and sycamore trees to Split Rock and the picnic area. Take the trail across the stream, heading out of the canyon to another stream crossing by sculptured volcanic rocks. Parallel the stream to a signed junction. Take the left fork—the Backbone Trail—curving uphill towards Inspiration

Point. A short side path leads up to the overlook. Continue east on the Backbone Trail to another junction. This side trail switchbacks up to the 360-degree views at Sandstone Peak. From the junction, it is 0.8 miles downhill back to the Mishe Mokwa junction, completing the loop.

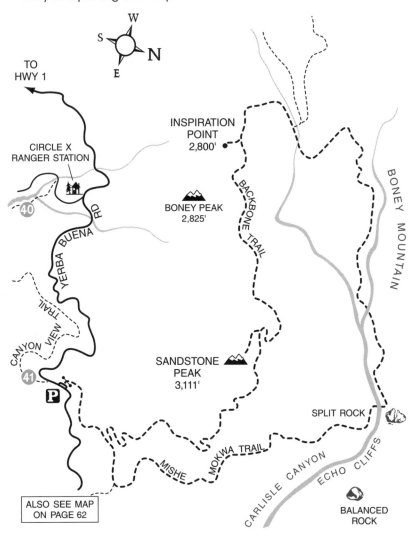

SANDSTONE PEAK LOOP
CIRCLE X RANCH

Hike 43
Lower Arroyo Sequit Trail and Sequit Point
LEO CARRILLO STATE BEACH

Hiking distance: 3 miles round trip
Hiking time: 1.5 hours
Elevation gain: 200 feet
Maps: U.S.G.S. Triunfo Pass
Leo Carrillo State Beach map

Summary of hike: Leo Carrillo State Beach is a 2,000-acre haven with a 1.5-mile stretch of coastline, mountain canyons, and steep chaparral covered hillsides. The area was once inhabited by the Chumash Indians. The Lower Arroyo Sequit Trail leads into a cool, stream-fed canyon shaded with willow, sycamore, oak, and bay trees. The path ends in the deep-walled canyon by large multicolored boulders and the trickling stream. At the oceanfront, Sequit Point, a rocky bluff, juts out from the shoreline, dividing North Beach from South Beach. The weather-carved point has sea caves and coves, sculpted arches, tidepools, and pocket beaches.

Driving directions: From the Pacific Coast Highway (Highway 1) and Las Posas Road in southeast Oxnard, drive 11.1 miles southbound on PCH to the posted Leo Carrillo State Beach entrance and turn left. Park in the day-use parking lot. A parking fee is required.

Heading northbound on the Pacific Coast Highway from Malibu, Leo Carrillo State Beach is on the right, 14 miles past Malibu Canyon Road and 8 miles past Kanan Dume Road.

Hiking directions: Hike north through the campground on the road past mature sycamores and oaks. Pass the amphitheater on the right to a gated road. Continue past the gate, crossing over the seasonal Arroyo Sequit to the end of the paved road. Take the footpath a hundred yards, and rock hop over the creek by a small grotto. Follow the path upstream along the east side of the creek. Recross the creek to the trail's end in a steep-walled box canyon with pools and large boulders. Retrace your steps to the amphitheater, and now bear left on the footpath. Cross to the east side of the creek and head through the forest canopy. Switchbacks and two sets of wooden steps lead to a flat above the canyon. Descend back to the campground road.

To reach Sequit Point, take the paved path under Highway 1 to the sandy beach. To the right (west), by the lifeguard station, are sandstone rock formations with caves, tunnels, a rock arch, tidepools, and a series of beach coves.

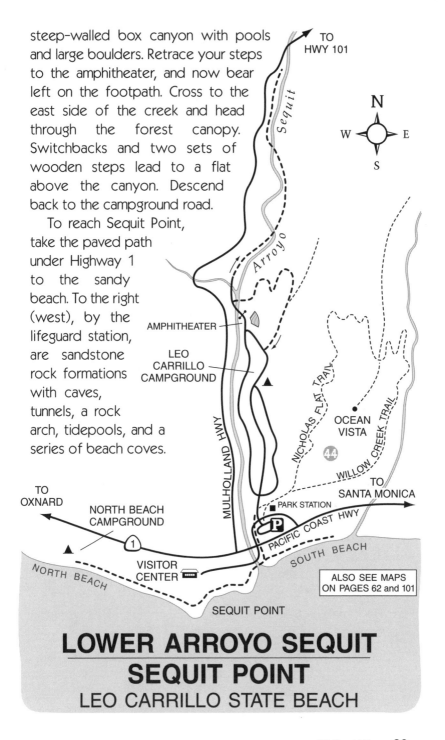

TO
HWY 101

N
W ← → E
S

Sequit

Arroyo

AMPHITHEATER

LEO
CARRILLO
CAMPGROUND

NICHOLAS FLAT TRAIL

WILLOW CREEK TRAIL

OCEAN
VISTA

44

MULHOLLAND HWY

TO
OXNARD

NORTH BEACH
CAMPGROUND

1

TO
SANTA MONICA

PARK STATION

PACIFIC COAST HWY

P

SOUTH BEACH

NORTH BEACH

VISITOR
CENTER

ALSO SEE MAPS
ON PAGES 62 and 101

SEQUIT POINT

LOWER ARROYO SEQUIT
SEQUIT POINT
LEO CARRILLO STATE BEACH

Hike 44
Nicholas Flat and Willow Creek Loop
LEO CARRILLO STATE BEACH

Hiking distance: 2.5 mile loop
Hiking time: 1.3 hours
Elevation gain: 612 feet
Maps: U.S.G.S. Triunfo Pass
Santa Monica Mountains West Trail Map
Leo Carrillo State Beach map

Summary of hike: This loop hike in Leo Carrillo State Beach leads to Ocean Vista, a 612-foot bald knoll with great views of the Malibu coastline and Point Dume. The Willow Creek Trail traverses the east-facing hillside up Willow Creek Canyon to Ocean Vista. The hike returns along the Nicholas Flat Trail, one of the few trails connecting the Santa Monica Mountains to the Pacific Ocean.

Driving directions: Same as Hike 43.

Hiking directions: The trailhead is 50 yards outside the park entrance station. Take the signed trail 100 yards northeast to a trail split. The loop begins at this junction. Take the right fork—the Willow Creek Trail—up the hillside and parallel to the ocean, heading east. At a half mile the trail curves north, traversing the hillside while overlooking the arroyo and Willow Creek. Three switchbacks lead aggressively up to a saddle and a signed four-way junction with the Nicholas Flat Trail. The left fork leads a quarter mile to Ocean Vista. After marveling at the views, return to the four-way junction and take the left (west) fork. Head downhill on the Nicholas Flat Trail across the grassy slopes above the park campground. Return to the junction near the trailhead.

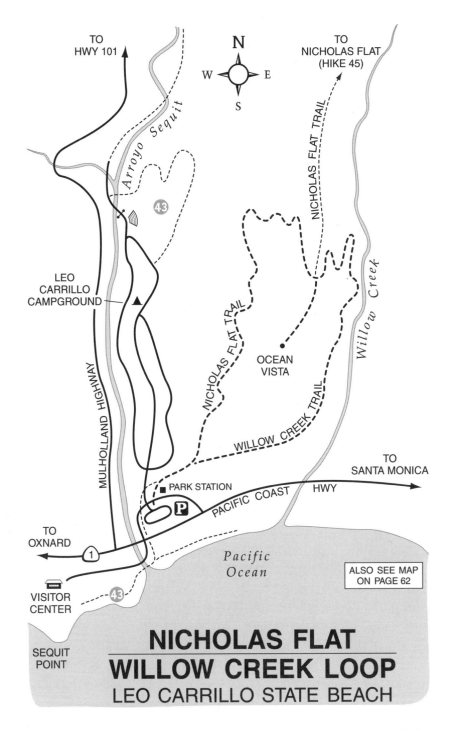

TO
HWY 101

N

W E

S

TO
NICHOLAS FLAT
(HIKE 45)

Arroyo Sequit

NICHOLAS FLAT TRAIL

43

LEO
CARRILLO
CAMPGROUND

Willow Creek

NICHOLAS FLAT TRAIL

OCEAN
VISTA

MULHOLLAND HIGHWAY

WILLOW CREEK TRAIL

TO
SANTA MONICA

■ PARK STATION

P

PACIFIC COAST HWY

TO
OXNARD

1

*Pacific
Ocean*

ALSO SEE MAP
ON PAGE 62

VISITOR
CENTER

43

SEQUIT
POINT

NICHOLAS FLAT
WILLOW CREEK LOOP
LEO CARRILLO STATE BEACH

Hike 45
Nicholas Flat
LEO CARRILLO STATE BEACH

Hiking distance: 2.5 mile double loop
Hiking time: 1.3 hours
Elevation gain: 100 feet
Maps: U.S.G.S. Triunfo Pass
Santa Monica Mountains West Trail Map
Leo Carrillo State Beach map

Summary of hike: Nicholas Flat, in the upper reaches of Leo Carrillo State Beach, is a grassy highland meadow with large oak trees, an old cattle pond, and sandstone outcroppings 1,700 feet above the sea. This hike skirts around Nicholas Flat with spectacular views of the ocean, San Nicholas Canyon, and the surrounding mountains. The Nicholas Flat Trail may be hiked 3.5 miles downhill to the Pacific Ocean, connecting to Hike 44.

Driving directions: From the Pacific Coast Highway (Highway 1) and Las Posas Road in southeast Oxnard, drive 13.3 miles southbound on PCH to Decker Road and turn left. Continue 2.4 miles north to Decker School Road and turn left. Drive 1.5 miles to the road's end and park alongside the road.
  Heading northbound on the Pacific Coast Highway from Malibu, Decker Road is on the right, 11.8 miles past Malibu Canyon Road and 5.8 miles past Kanan Dume Road.

Hiking directions: Hike south past the gate and kiosk. Stay on the wide, oak-lined trail to a junction at 0.3 miles. Take the right fork, beginning the first loop. At 0.6 miles is another junction. Again take the right fork—the Meadows Trail. Continue past the Malibu Springs Trail on the right to Vista Point, where there are great views into the canyons. The trail curves south to a junction with the Nicholas Flat Trail, leading to Leo Carrillo State Beach. Take the left fork around the perimeter of the flat. A trail on the right leads to another vista point. Complete the first loop at 1.8 miles. Take the trail to the right at two successive junctions to a pond. Follow along the pond through the meadow, completing the second loop. Return to the trailhead.

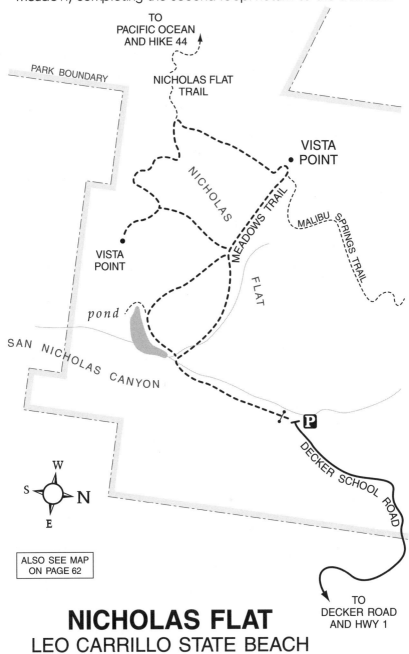

TO PACIFIC OCEAN AND HIKE 44

PARK BOUNDARY

NICHOLAS FLAT TRAIL

VISTA POINT

NICHOLAS

MEADOWS TRAIL

MALIBU SPRINGS TRAIL

VISTA POINT

FLAT

pond

SAN NICHOLAS CANYON

P

DECKER SCHOOL ROAD

W
S ⊕ N
E

ALSO SEE MAP
ON PAGE 62

TO DECKER ROAD AND HWY 1

NICHOLAS FLAT
LEO CARRILLO STATE BEACH

Hike 46
Arroyo Sequit Park

Hiking distance: 2 mile loop
Hiking time: 1 hour
Elevation gain: 250 feet
Maps: U.S.G.S. Triunfo Pass
Santa Monica Mountains West Trail Map

Summary of hike: Arroyo Sequit Park was a ranch purchased by the Santa Monica Mountains Conservancy in 1985. Within the 155-acre park boundary are open grassland meadows, picnic areas, and a small canyon cut by the East Fork Arroyo Sequit, with oak groves and a waterfall. From the meadows are panoramic views of the ocean and surrounding mountains. This easy loop hike visits the diverse park habitats, crossing the meadows and dropping into the gorge that runs parallel to the East Fork Arroyo Sequit.

Driving directions: From the Pacific Coast Highway (Highway 1) and Las Posas Road in southeast Oxnard, drive 10.8 miles southbound on PCH to Mulholland Highway. Turn left and drive 5.5 miles up the canyon to the signed turnoff on the right at mailbox 34138. Turn right into the park entrance.

Heading northbound on the Pacific Coast Highway from Malibu, Mulholland Highway is 8.5 miles past Kanan Dume Road and 0.3 miles past the Leo Carrillo State Beach entrance.

Hiking directions: Head south on the park road past the gate, kiosk, and old ranch house. At 0.2 miles take the road to the left—past a barn, the astronomical observing site, and picnic area—to the footpath on the right. Leave the service road on the nature trail, heading south. The trail skirts the east edge of the meadow, then descends into a small canyon and crosses several seasonal tributaries of the Arroyo Sequit. Head west along the southern wall of the canyon, passing a waterfall on the left. Cross a wooden footbridge over the stream, and descend to the canyon floor. Continue west, cross the East

Fork Arroyo Sequit, and begin the ascent out of the canyon to a junction. Continue straight ahead up the hill. A series of switchbacks lead up the short but steep hill. Once at the top, cross the meadow to the road. Take the service road back to the parking area.

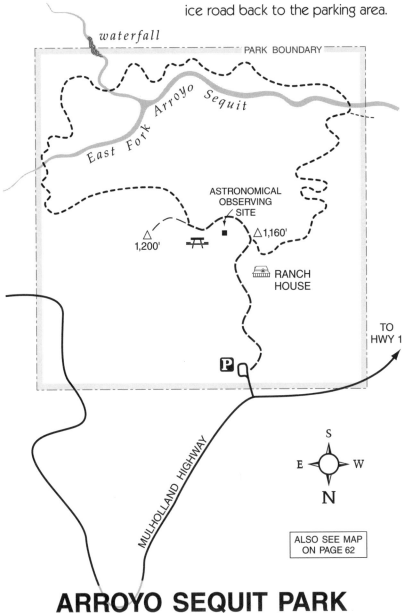

waterfall

PARK BOUNDARY

East Fork Arroyo Sequit

ASTRONOMICAL
OBSERVING
SITE

△ 1,200'

🏕 RANCH
HOUSE

△ 1,160'

TO
HWY 1

P

MULHOLLAND HIGHWAY

S
E ← ⊕ → W
N

ALSO SEE MAP
ON PAGE 62

ARROYO SEQUIT PARK

Hike 47
Charmlee County Park
Open 8:00 a.m. to sunset daily

Hiking distance: 3 mile loop
Hiking time: 1.5 hours
Elevation gain: 600 feet
Maps: U.S.G.S. Triunfo Pass
Santa Monica Mountains West Trail Map
City of Malibu—Charmlee Natural Area map

Summary of hike: Perched on oceanfront cliffs 1,300 feet above the sea, Charmlee County Park has a magnificent bird's-eye view of the Malibu coastline. The 460-acre wilderness park was an old cattle ranch that was purchased by Los Angeles County in 1968 and opened as a county park in 1981. A network of interconnecting footpaths and old ranch roads weave through expansive grassy meadows, oak and eucalyptus woodlands, mountain slopes, rocky ridges, and 1,250-foot bluffs overlooking the sea. The park has picnic areas and a nature center with plant exhibits.

Driving directions: From the Pacific Coast Highway (Highway 1) and Las Posas Road in southeast Oxnard, drive 14 miles southbound on PCH to Encinal Canyon Road and turn left. Continue 3.7 miles to the Charmlee Park entrance on the left. Follow the park road 0.2 miles to the parking lot.
   Heading northbound on the Pacific Coast Highway from Malibu, Encinal Canyon Road is 11.2 miles past Malibu Canyon Road and 5.2 miles past Kanan Dume Road.

Hiking directions: Hike past the information board and picnic area on the wide trail. Pass a second picnic area on the left in an oak grove, and continue uphill to a three-way trail split. The middle trail is a short detour leading to an overlook set among rock formations and an old house foundation. Take the main trail to the left into the large grassy meadow. Two trails cross the meadow and rejoin at the south end—the main trail heads through the meadow while the right fork skirts the meadow's western edge. At the far end is an ocean overlook and a trail fork. Bear left past an old ranch reservoir. Continue downhill, curving north through an oak grove to the unsigned Botany Trail, a narrow footpath on the right. The Botany Trail winds back to the picnic area and the trailhead.

OVERLOOKS

reservoir

PARK BOUNDARY

LECHUSA CANYON

MEADOW

OVERLOOK

BOTANY TRAIL

NATURE CENTER

P

ENCINAL CANYON ROAD

S

E — W

N

ALSO SEE MAP
ON PAGE 62

TO
HWY 1

CHARMLEE COUNTY PARK

Hike 48
Newton Canyon Falls
ZUMA/TRANCAS CANYONS: Upper Zuma Canyon

Hiking distance: 1.5 miles round trip
Hiking time: 1 hour
Elevation gain: 200 feet
Maps: U.S.G.S. Point Dume
      Santa Monica Mountains West Trail Map

Summary of hike: The Upper Zuma Canyon Trail begins in Newton Canyon. The trail leads a short distance along a portion of the Backbone Trail to Newton Canyon Falls, a year-round, 30-foot waterfall in a lush, forested grotto with mossy rocks and a tangle of vines. There are large, shaded boulders to sit on near the falls by cascading Newton Creek.

Driving directions: From Highway 101 (Ventura Freeway) in Agoura Hills, exit on Kanan Road. Drive 7.9 miles south to the trailhead parking lot on the right. The parking lot is located just before entering the third tunnel (T-1). (Kanan Road becomes Kanan Dume Road after it crosses Mulholland Highway.)
    From Santa Monica, drive 18 miles northbound on the Pacific Coast Highway (Highway 1) to Kanan Dume Road, 5.8 miles past Malibu Canyon Road. Turn right and drive 4.4 miles north to the trailhead parking lot on the left. The parking lot is located just after going through the first tunnel (T-1).

Hiking directions: Hike west, away from Kanan Dume Road, on the signed Backbone Trail. The trail immediately begins its descent from the open chaparral into the shady canyon. After crossing the trickling Newton Creek, a side trail on the left leads 20 yards to sandstone rocks at the top of the falls. The main trail continues 100 yards downhill to a second cutoff trail on the left. Take this steep side path downhill through a forest of oaks, sycamores, and bay laurels to the creek, bearing to the left on the descent. Once at the creek, hike upstream along the path. Fifty yards up the narrow canyon is a lush grotto at the base of Newton Canyon Falls. The main trail continues west into the rugged Zuma Canyon with steep volcanic cliffs. After enjoying the waterfall, return by retracing your steps.

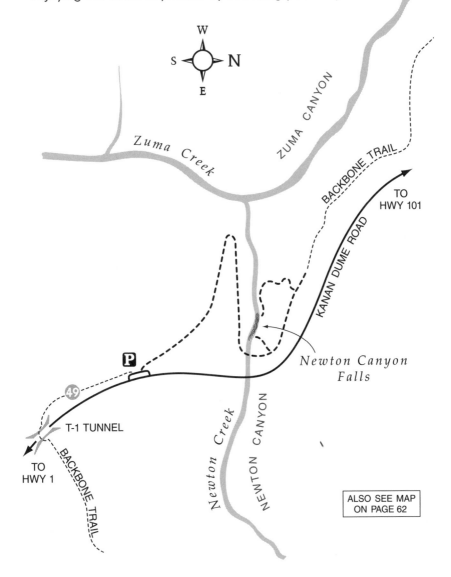

NEWTON CANYON FALLS
ZUMA/TRANCAS CANYONS

Hike 49
Newton Canyon
ZUMA / TRANCAS CANYONS

Hiking distance: 4.6 miles round trip
Hiking time: 2.5 hours
Elevation gain: 300 feet
Maps: U.S.G.S. Point Dume
Santa Monica Mountains West Trail Map

Summary of hike: This hike parallels Newton Canyon along a 2.3-mile portion of the Backbone Trail between Kanan Dume Road and Latigo Canyon Road. The forested trail winds along the south ridge of the dense oak-filled canyon with ocean views and seasonal stream crossings.

Driving directions: From Highway 101 (Ventura Freeway) in Agoura Hills, exit on Kanan Road. Drive 7.9 miles south to the trailhead parking lot on the right. The parking lot is located just before entering the third tunnel (T-1). (Kanan Road becomes Kanan Dume Road after it crosses Mulholland Highway.)
From Santa Monica, drive 18 miles northbound on the Pacific Coast Highway (Highway 1) to Kanan Dume Road, 5.8 miles past Malibu Canyon Road. Turn right and drive 4.4 miles north to the trailhead parking lot on the left. The parking lot is located just after going through the first tunnel (T-1).

Hiking directions: The signed trail begins by Kanan Dume Road and heads south towards the ocean. The trail, an old fire road, climbs up to the tunnel and crosses over Kanan Dume Road. After crossing, the road narrows to a footpath and enters a forested canopy, slowly descending into the canyon. The trail crosses a paved driveway, then climbs to various over-looks. Continue along the winding mountainside above Newton Canyon. Near the end of the trail, a maze-like series of switch-backs lead to Latigo Canyon Road. This is the turnaround spot.
To hike further, cross the road to the trailhead parking area, and continue on the Backbone Trail. It is another 1.4 miles to

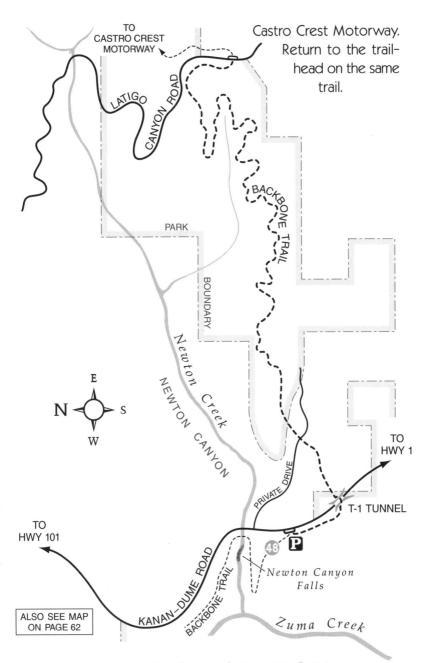

TO CASTRO CREST MOTORWAY

Castro Crest Motorway. Return to the trail-head on the same trail.

LATIGO CANYON ROAD

BACKBONE TRAIL

PARK

BOUNDARY

Newton Creek

NEWTON CANYON

E
N ◇ S
W

TO HWY 1

PRIVATE DRIVE

T-1 TUNNEL

TO HWY 101

48 P

Newton Canyon Falls

KANAN-DUME ROAD

BACKBONE TRAIL

ALSO SEE MAP ON PAGE 62

Zuma Creek

NEWTON CANYON
ZUMA/TRANCAS CANYONS

Hike 50
Rocky Oaks Park

Hiking distance: 2 mile loop
Hiking time: 1 hour
Elevation gain: 200 feet
Maps: U.S.G.S. Point Dume
      Santa Monica Mountains West Trail Map
      N.P.S. Rocky Oaks Site

Summary of hike: Rocky Oaks Park was once a working cattle ranch resting at the head of Zuma Canyon. The pastoral 200-acre ranch was purchased by the National Park Service in 1981. The park includes oak savannahs, rolling grasslands, chaparral covered hills, volcanic rock formations, scenic overlooks, picnic areas, and a pond in the grassy meadow. This easy loop hike meanders through the park, visiting each of these diverse ecological communities.

Driving directions: From Highway 101 (Ventura Freeway) in Agoura Hills, exit on Kanan Road. Drive 6.1 miles south to Mulholland Highway. Turn right and a quick right again into Rocky Oaks Park and the parking lot.

From Santa Monica, drive 18 miles northbound on the Pacific Coast Highway (Highway 1) to Kanan Dume Road, 5.8 miles past Malibu Canyon Road. Turn right and drive 6.2 miles north to Mulholland Highway. Turn left, then quickly turn right into the park entrance.

Hiking directions: Hike north past the rail fence to the Rocky Oaks Loop Trail, which heads in both directions. Take the left fork a short distance to a 4-way junction. Continue straight ahead on the middle path towards the Overlook Trail. Ascend the hillside overlooking the pond, and take the horseshoe bend to the left. Beyond the bend is the Overlook Trail. This is a short detour on the left to a scenic overlook with panoramic views. Back on the main trail, continue northeast around the ridge, slowly descending to the valley floor near Kanan Road. Bear sharply to the right, heading south to the Pond Trail junction. Both the left and right forks loop around the pond and rejoin at the south end. At the junction, go south and back to the Rocky Oaks Loop, then retrace your steps back to the trailhead.

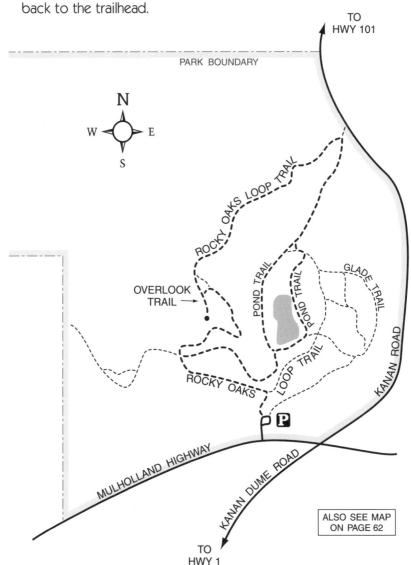

ROCKY OAKS PARK

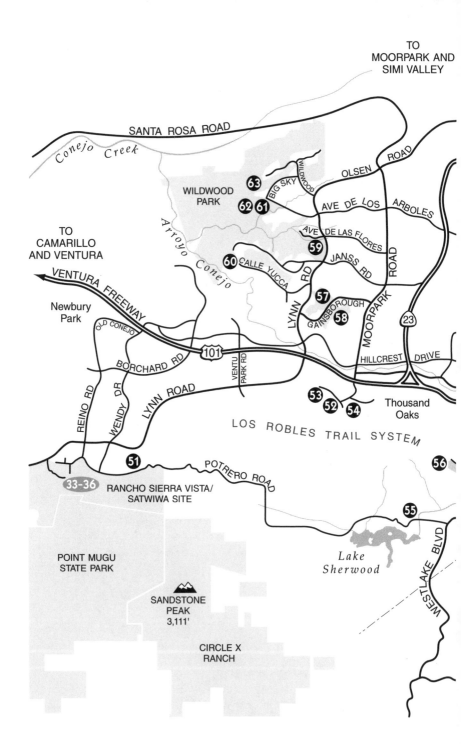

TO
MOORPARK AND
SIMI VALLEY

SANTA ROSA ROAD

Conejo Creek

WILDWOOD
PARK

63

62 61

BIG SKY

WILDWOOD

OLSEN ROAD

AVE DE LOS ARBOLES

Arroyo Conejo

TO
CAMARILLO
AND VENTURA

AVE DE LAS FLORES

59

60 CALLE YUCCA

LYNN RD

JANSS RD

MOORPARK ROAD

VENTURA FREEWAY

Newbury
Park

57

GAINSBOROUGH

58

23

OLD CONEJO

101

HILLCREST DRIVE

BORCHARD RD

VENTU PARK RD

REINO RD

WENDY DR

LYNN ROAD

53 52 54

Thousand
Oaks

LOS ROBLES TRAIL SYSTEM

51

POTRERO ROAD

56

33-36 RANCHO SIERRA VISTA/
SATWIWA SITE

55

POINT MUGU
STATE PARK

Lake
Sherwood

WESTLAKE BLVD

SANDSTONE
PEAK
3,111'

CIRCLE X
RANCH

THOUSAND OAKS
OAK PARK • AGOURA HILLS

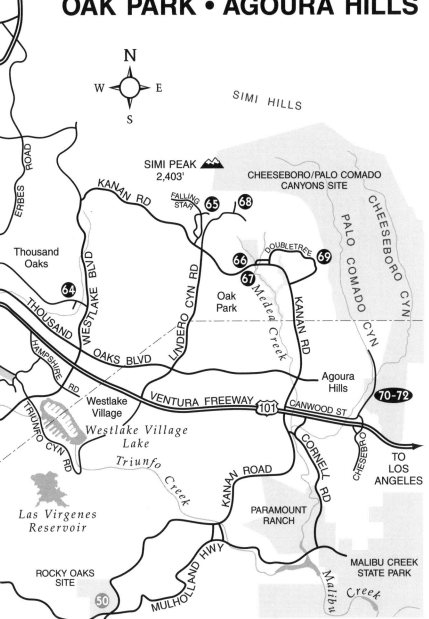

Hike 51
Los Robles Trail
POTRERO GATE TO ANGEL VISTA

Hiking distance: 5 miles round trip
Hiking time: 2.5 hours
Elevation gain: 500 feet
Maps: U.S.G.S. Newbury Park
Santa Monica Mountains West Trail Map
Los Robles Trail to Lake Sherwood map

map
next page

Summary of hike: The Los Robles Trail System is a well-planned network of trails weaving through the growing residential communities of Westlake Village, Thousand Oaks, and Newbury Park. The multi-use trails link the open spaces of the inland valley with Point Mugu State Park and the oceanfront Santa Monica Mountains. This is an important wildlife corridor connecting the Santa Monica Range with the Simi Hills. The hike from Potrero Gate follows an east-west ridge through oak woodlands and open chaparral to Angel Vista, a 1,600-foot overlook with sweeping bird's-eye views of Conejo Valley, Hidden Valley, and the surrounding mountains to the sea. Hikes 51 and 52 may be combined for a 6-mile, one-way shuttle hike.

Driving directions: From Highway 101 (Ventura Freeway) in Newbury Park, exit on Wendy Drive. Drive 2.7 miles south to Potrero Road. Turn left and go 0.5 miles to the posted trailhead parking area on the left.

Hiking directions: Walk up the hill past the trailhead kiosk to a paved, private road. Cross the road and curve right 100 yards to a Y-fork. Veer left and drop down the hill, curving to the right. Follow the undulating path parallel to Lynn Road on the open rolling hills. The trail slowly descends to the open space boundary behind homes fronting Lynn Road. Curve away from civilization, returning to the tall brush and rolling hills, to a posted junction on a saddle at 1.2 miles. The left fork descends to Felton Street at Lynn Road. Bear right and climb just shy of the ridge. Follow the rail fence through a private property easement, passing horse stables and corrals on the left. Cross the saddle and drop into the adjacent draw to the east. Four switchbacks zigzag up the hillside to a Y-junction at 2.5 miles. The right fork descends 3.5 miles to Moorpark Road (Hike 52), which can be hiked as a 6-mile, one-way shuttle. For this hike, take the Rosewood Trail to the left, quickly reaching another fork. The trail to the right continues 1.8 miles downhill to Lynn Road near the Stagecoach Inn Museum. Bear left 0.1 mile to Angel Vista, an overlook and picnic bench at the summit. Return by retracing your route.

Hike 52
Los Robles Trail
MOORPARK GATE TO ANGEL VISTA

Hiking distance: 7.2 miles round trip
Hiking time: 3.5 hours

map next page

Elevation gain: 700 feet
Maps: U.S.G.S. Newbury Park
Santa Monica Mountains West Trail Map
Los Robles Trail to Lake Sherwood map

Summary of hike: The Los Robles Trail System is a network of paths that connects the area's open spaces and undeveloped areas with Westlake Village, Thousand Oaks, and Newbury Park. The multi-use trails are thoughtfully blended with the encroaching residential areas, linking several inland valleys with the Santa Monica Mountains at Point Mugu State Park. This hike heads west on the Los Robles Trail from Moorpark Gate to Angel Vista, a 1,600-foot overlook with sweeping 360-degree vistas that span across Conejo Valley, the Santa Susana and Topatopa Mountains, and seaward to the Channel Islands.

Driving directions: From Highway 101 (Ventura Freeway) in Thousand Oaks, exit on Moorpark Road and drive 0.5 miles south to Greenmeadow Avenue. Cross through the intersection and park on the right in the posted trailhead parking area.

Hiking directions: Walk past the trailhead gate to a trail fork at 100 yards. Stay to the right and pass the Oak Creek Canyon Trail on the right (Hike 53). Continue to a trail split with the Los Robles Trail heading east at 0.4 miles. Again, stay to the right on the Los Robles Trail heading west, passing a junction with the Spring Canyon Trail. Cross the rolling terrain through chaparral to the base of the hills. Short, steep switchbacks climb from the lower reaches of the hillside to the ridge. At 2 miles, cross a saddle and follow the contours of the hillside, dipping into the canyon while overlooking the landscape of Thousand Oaks and Newbury Park. Zigzag down two switch-

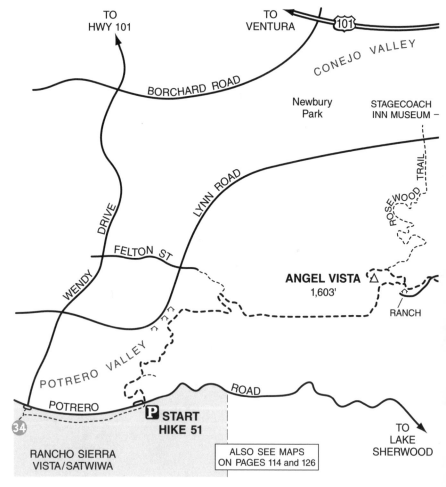

backs on the brush-shaded path to an unpaved, private extension of Ventu Park Road at just under 3 miles. Cross the road and climb again, skirting the edge of a ranch. Continue through the tall brush to a posted junction with the Rosewood Trail at 3.5 miles. The left fork (Hike 51) descends 2.5 miles to Potrero Road, across from the Rancho Sierra Vista/Satwiwa site. Take the Rosewood Trail to the right, quickly reaching another fork. The Rosewood Trail continues 1.8 miles downhill to Lynn Road, just west of Ventu Park Road. Bear left 0.1 mile to Angel Vista, an overlook and picnic bench at the summit. After enjoying the vistas, return by retracing your steps.

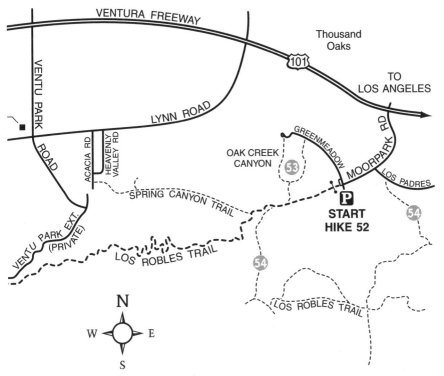

HIKES 51 • 52
LOS ROBLES TRAIL
PORTRERO GATE TO ANGEL VISTA
MOORPARK GATE TO ANGEL VISTA

Hike 53
Oak Creek Canyon
LOS ROBLES TRAIL SYSTEM

Hiking distance: 0.8 mile loop
Hiking time: 45 minutes
Elevation gain: 100 feet
Maps: U.S.G.S. Newbury Park
Santa Monica Mountains West Trail Map
Los Robles Trail to Lake Sherwood map

Summary of hike: The Oak Creek Canyon Trail is a short hike through a gorgeous oak woodland just minutes from the heart of Thousand Oaks. The forested pathway links to the extensive Los Robles Trail System. The first quarter mile of the hike meanders through the Oak Creek Canyon Whole Access Trail, an interpretive trail with learning stations and a guide wire to assist the blind. The text at each station is written in English and Braille, describing the immediate surroundings through touch, smell, and sound. The trail continues on the Oak Creek Canyon Loop through chaparral covered hills, looping back to Greenmeadow Avenue.

Driving directions: From Highway 101 (Ventura Freeway) in Thousand Oaks, exit on Moorpark Road. Drive 0.5 miles south to Greenmeadow Avenue—turn right. Continue 0.4 miles to the road's end and the trailhead parking lot at the Arts Council Center.

Hiking directions: From the parking lot, walk to the left (south) past the kiosk and restrooms. The trail begins in the forested canopy along a wooden fence. At the end of the quarter-mile Whole Access Trail, pass through the fence to the Oak Creek Canyon Loop. A short distance ahead is a junction. The right fork connects to the Los Robles Trail (Hikes 52 and 54). Take the left fork, looping back to the north. At 0.3 miles, the trail connects with Greenmeadow Avenue. The parking lot is a short distance along the road to the left. Return on the road for a 0.8-mile loop, or retrace your steps to the trailhead.

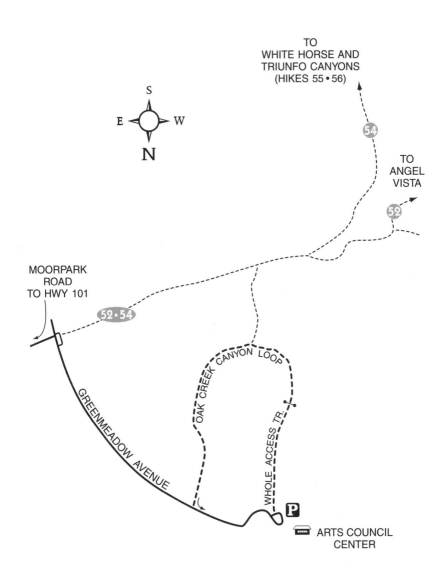

TO
WHITE HORSE AND
TRIUNFO CANYONS
(HIKES 55 • 56)

S
E · W
N

TO
ANGEL
VISTA

54

52

MOORPARK
ROAD
TO HWY 101

52 · 54

OAK CREEK CANYON LOOP

GREENMEADOW AVENUE

OAK CREEK CANYON TR.

WHOLE ACCESS TR.

P

ARTS COUNCIL
CENTER

ALSO SEE MAPS
ON PAGES 114 and 118

OAK CREEK CANYON
LOS ROBLES TRAIL SYSTEM

Hike 54
Los Padres—Los Robles Loop
LOS ROBLES TRAIL SYSTEM

Hiking distance: 3.5 mile loop
Hiking time: 1.5 hours
Elevation gain: 400 feet
Maps: U.S.G.S. Newbury Park
Santa Monica Mountains West Trail Map
Los Robles Trail to Lake Sherwood map

Summary of hike: The Los Padres Trail winds through an oak woodland with a seasonal stream, then joins the main Los Robles Trail on a ridge. The hike follows the ridge across an open highland meadow with unobstructed views overlooking Hidden Valley and Conejo Valley. This loop trail lies just south of Thousand Oaks and Oak Creek Canyon (Hike 53).

Driving directions: From Highway 101 (Ventura Freeway) in Thousand Oaks, exit on Moorpark Road. Drive 0.4 miles south to Los Padres Drive and turn left. Continue 100 yards and park by the trailhead gate on the right, located across the street from Woodlet Way.

Hiking directions: Take the trail south past the Los Padres Trailhead sign and gate through the oak forest. The trail parallels, then crosses, a seasonal stream. After crossing, begin a gradual but steady ascent, zigzagging from the canyon floor to the junction with the Los Robles Trail. Take the wide, signed trail to the right, continuing uphill to a junction at the top of the hill by a bench above the valley. Bear to the right, staying on the Los Robles Trail. In a quarter mile is a junction with the Scenic Overlook Loop on the right. Take this short trail through the open meadow, overlooking Thousand Oaks and the Conejo Valley. After rejoining the Los Robles Trail, take the path downhill to the right. At the bottom are two trail splits. Bear to the right each time, following the signs to Moorpark Road. Pass the trails on the left to Angel Vista (Hike 52) and Oak Creek Canyon

(Hike 53). The trail exits at Moorpark Road. Walk one block and turn right at Los Padres Drive, returning to the trailhead.

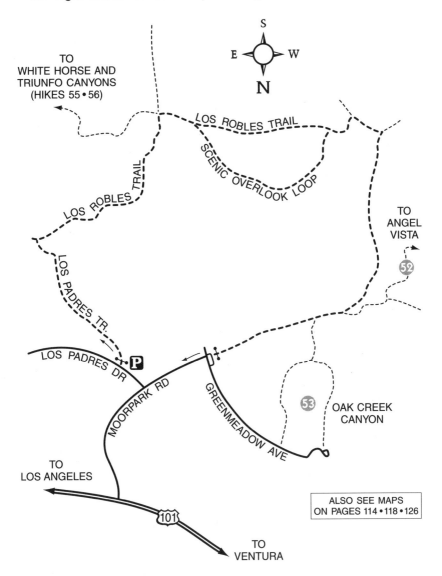

LOS PADRES–LOS ROBLES LOOP
LOS ROBLES TRAIL SYSTEM

Hike 55
White Horse Canyon Trail
LOS ROBLES TRAIL SYSTEM

Hiking distance: 3.5 mile loop
Hiking time: 1.5 hours
Elevation gain: 500 feet
Maps: U.S.G.S. Thousand Oaks
       Santa Monica Mountains West Trail Map
       Los Robles Trail to Lake Sherwood map

map next page

Summary of hike: The White Horse Canyon Trail, near the east end of the Los Robles Trail System, loops around the rolling, chaparral covered foothills to a ridge overlooking Westlake Village and Thousand Oaks. There is an overlook with a panoramic view of Lake Sherwood, the cliffs above Hidden Valley, and the Santa Monica Mountains.

Driving directions: From Highway 101 (Ventura Freeway) in Thousand Oaks, exit on Westlake Boulevard. Drive 1.8 miles south to East Potrero Road and turn right. Continue 0.5 miles and park on the right across from the Foxfield Riding Club, just beyond the bridge over Potrero Valley Creek.

Hiking directions: From the parking area, the trailhead and kiosk are across the creekbed to the north. Head up the hill, past the homes on the right, to a fire road. The fire road leads to a junction. The left fork is a short side trip to a scenic overlook of Lake Sherwood. Back at the junction, take the north fork 0.5 miles to another junction with the White Horse Canyon Trail on the left. This footpath loops around the back side of the canyon before rejoining the fire road. Take the road to the right uphill a short distance to a junction with the Conejo Crest Trail on the left. Head left along the ridge as it descends back down to Potrero Valley Creek. Cross the creekbed into the park. Take the park path to the right, leading back to the parking area.

Hike 56
Triunfo Canyon Trail
LOS ROBLES TRAIL SYSTEM

Hiking distance: 2.5 mile loop
Hiking time: 1 hour
Elevation gain: 400 feet
Maps: U.S.G.S. Thousand Oaks
Santa Monica Mountains West Trail Map
Los Robles Trail to Lake Sherwood map

map next page

Summary of hike: The Triunfo Canyon Trail is part of the open space area near Westlake Village. The hike follows Triunfo Canyon from Triunfo Community Park to rolling grasslands on the ridge, connecting with the Los Robles Trail. Atop the ridge are sweeping vistas of Westlake Village, the Conejo and Russell Valleys, Lake Sherwood, and the Santa Monica Mountains.

Driving directions: From Highway 101 (Ventura Freeway) in Thousand Oaks, exit on Hampshire Road. Drive 0.6 miles south to Triunfo Canyon Road and turn right. Continue 0.5 miles to Tamarack Street and turn right. The trailhead is 0.2 miles ahead in the parking lot at the north end of Triunfo Community Park.

Hiking directions: From the parking lot, head northwest on the signed trail past the kiosk. The trail gradually climbs along the contours of Triunfo Canyon to the ridgeline. Near the top, a short series of steep switchbacks lead to a bench. From the bench are great views of the valley below. The trail then levels out to a junction with the Los Robles Trail—go to the left. Thirty feet ahead is a ridge with views of the mountains and another junction. Take the signed Los Robles Trail South to the left to a third trail split. Proceed downhill on the left fork. The trail ends at Brookview Avenue. Walk through the neighborhood one block to Stonesgate Street. Go to the left and proceed one block to Aranmoor Avenue. Go left again, returning to the park. The park path heads left, leading back to the parking lot.

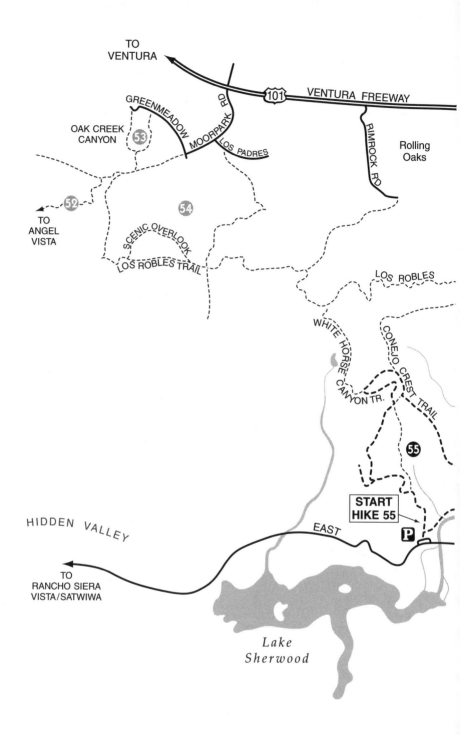

TO
VENTURA

101 VENTURA FREEWAY

GREENMEADOW

MOORPARK RD

LOS PADRES

RIMROCK RD

OAK CREEK
CANYON (53)

Rolling
Oaks

(52)

TO
ANGEL
VISTA

(54)

SCENIC OVERLOOK

LOS ROBLES TRAIL

LOS ROBLES

WHITE HORSE CANYON TR.

CONEJO CREST TRAIL

(55)

START
HIKE 55

P

HIDDEN VALLEY

EAST

TO
RANCHO SIERA
VISTA/SATWIWA

Lake
Sherwood

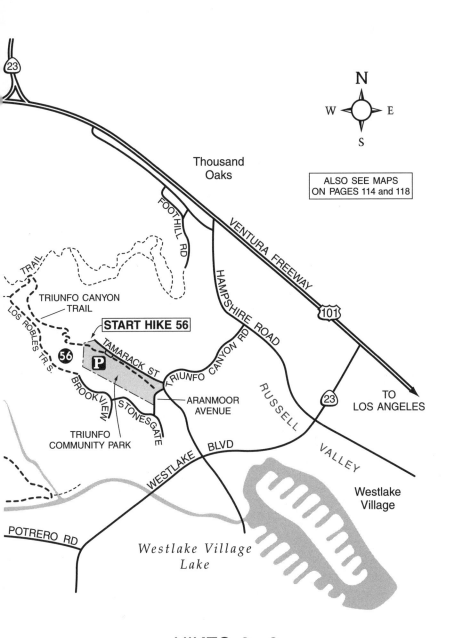

HIKES 8 • 9
WHITE HORSE CANYON
TRIUNFO CANYON

Hike 57
Dawn's Peak

Hiking distance: 1 mile round trip
Hiking time: 30 minutes
Elevation gain: 250 feet
Maps: U.S.G.S. Newbury Park

Summary of hike: Dawn's Peak, also known as Tarantula Hill, is a 400-foot rounded mound in Thousand Oaks across from the Conejo Valley Botanic Garden (Hike 58) and Community Park. The trail spirals up the mound. From the 1,057-foot summit are 360-degree panoramic vistas of Thousand Oaks and the surrounding mountains.

Driving directions: From Highway 101 (Ventura Freeway) in Thousand Oaks, exit on Lynn Road and drive 0.6 miles north to Gainsborough Road. Turn right and continue 0.5 miles to the posted Conejo Valley Botanic Garden entrance. (Dawn's Peak is the rounded mound on the left.) Turn right and park in the lot on the left, 0.2 miles ahead.

Hiking directions: Walk a quarter mile up the entrance road back to Gainsborough Road. Cross the street to the dirt path. Walk up the path to the southern base of Dawn's Peak. Take the paved vehicle-restricted service road to the left, and loop back to the right, walking in a counter-clockwise direction. The road corkscrews up the hill, gaining elevation with every step and continuously changing views. At the summit is a fenced water company facility. A footpath circles the peak with a south-facing bench to enjoy the great close-up views of Thousand Oaks, the Santa Monica Mountains, Wildwood Park, and the Simi Hills. Return by retracing your steps.

To extend the hike, continue through the Conejo Valley Botanic Garden (Hike 58).

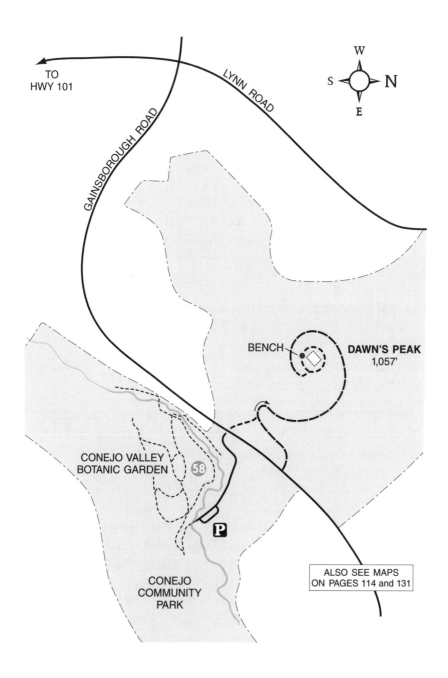

TO
HWY 101

LYNN ROAD

GAINSBOROUGH ROAD

W

S —◆— N

E

BENCH —● **DAWN'S PEAK**
1,057'

CONEJO VALLEY
BOTANIC GARDEN   **58**

P

CONEJO
COMMUNITY
PARK

ALSO SEE MAPS
ON PAGES 114 and 131

DAWN'S PEAK

Hike 58
Conejo Valley Botanic Garden

Hiking distance: 1.5 miles round trip
Hiking time: 1 hour
Elevation gain: 100 feet
Maps: U.S.G.S. Newbury Park
      Conejo Valley Botanic Garden map

Summary of hike: The Conejo Valley Botanic Garden in Thousand Oaks encompasses 33 acres. The garden's meandering paths lead past native plants and fruit trees and include sections of desert, Mediterranean, herb, and butterfly gardens. From the gardens, a nature trail follows a creek in a natural canyon filled with oaks and willows.

Driving directions: From Highway 101 (Ventura Freeway) in Thousand Oaks, exit on Lynn Road. Head 0.6 miles north to Gainsborough Road and turn right. Continue 0.5 miles to the Conejo Valley Botanic Garden entrance and turn right. The parking lot is 0.2 miles ahead on the left.

Hiking directions: From the parking lot, walk to the end of the road to the botanic garden entrance. Hike up the pathway into Conejo Community Park. A sign directs you to the right into the garden to an information kiosk and trail junction. Take the left fork on the upper trail to another junction. Steps lead straight ahead to benches and overlooks. Many interconnecting trails lead to various overlooks. There are numerous garden paths. The nature trail descends into a forested canyon to a junction by the creek. The left fork leads deeper into the canyon and crosses a wooden bridge over the creek. The right fork crosses the creek. In both cases, reverse the route to return. After enjoying the gardens, return to the parking lot.

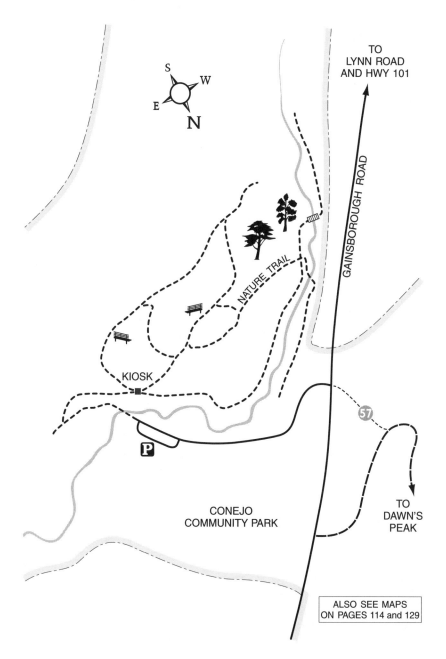

CONEJO VALLEY
BOTANIC GARDEN

Hike 59
Lynnmere—Wildwood Canyon Loop (East Side)
WILDWOOD PARK

Hiking distance: 4 mile loop
Hiking time: 2 hours
Elevation gain: 500 feet
Maps: U.S.G.S. Newbury Park
Wildwood Park Trail Guide

map
next page

Summary of hikes 59 and 60: Wildwood Park, in Thousand Oaks, is an immense 1,700-acre park with 27 miles of hiking trails. The diverse terrain includes volcanic rock formations, several canyons with riparian and oak-shaded woodlands, two year-round streams, and two waterfalls. The Lynnmere Trail crosses from one end of Wildwood Park to the other, following the rolling terrain above Wildwood Canyon. The hillside path connects with the canyon bottom trails at Arroyo Conejo Creek and the North Fork of Arroyo Conejo Creek. Hike 59 loops through the east end of Wildwood Park, traversing the chaparral covered ridge and lush gullies, then returning along the North Fork through a deep rock canyon. Hike 60 descends into lush Arroyo Conejo Canyon under the shade of coastal live oaks. The path follows Arroyo Conejo Creek and returns along the North Fork in Wildwood Canyon. The hike includes a visit to Paradise Falls (back cover photo).

Driving directions: From Highway 101 (Ventura Freeway) in Thousand Oaks, exit on Lynn Road and drive 2.2 miles north to Avenida De Las Flores. Turn left and park.

Hiking directions: Walk back to Lynn Road, and go to the right 0.2 miles to a footpath on the right, across from Sidlee Street. Bear right and ascend the knoll, traversing the chaparral covered ridge. Gradual descend to the canyon floor, and cross the stream to an unmarked junction. Stay on the main trail, heading up the hill. The undulating path climbs over dry ridges and dips into lush drainages. Cross a footbridge to a junction. The left fork follows a wide, grassy draw 150 yards to Lynnmere Drive, just east of Watertown Court. Take the grassy path to the right, down to the canyon bottom. Cross the North Fork Arroyo Conejo Creek, upstream from Paradise Falls, to the Wildwood Canyon Trail. To the left is Paradise Falls (Hike 61). Bear right, following the North Fork upstream. Cross a bridge over the creek on the right, staying on the Wildwood Canyon Trail. Meander along the creek through a shady rock-walled canyon, passing sculpted rock formations and pools. Cross another footbridge to the north side of the creek and a posted junction. Stay to the right and cross the creek again. Ascend the wide, eroded path, and traverse the hill along the park boundary to the entrance gate at Avenida De Las Flores. Continue along the road for two blocks, completing the loop.

Hike 60
Lynnmere—Arroyo Conejo—
Wildwood Canyon Loop (West Side)
WILDWOOD PARK

Hiking distance: 4.5 mile loop
Hiking time: 2.5 hours
Elevation gain: 500 feet
Maps: U.S.G.S. Newbury Park
Wildwood Park Trail Guide

map
next page

Summary of hike: See previous hike.

Driving directions: From Highway 101 (Ventura Freeway) in Thousand Oaks, exit on Lynn Road and drive 1.3 miles north to Camino Manzanas. Turn left and continue 0.4 miles to Calle Yucca. Turn right and go 1.1 mile to the gate at the end of the street and park. The trailhead is on the left

Hiking directions: Take the distinct trail a short distance west to a trail split. The right fork is our return route. Cross the concrete water channel and veer to the left. A long, steady descent leads to an attractive grove of coastal live oaks at the canyon floor. Under the shaded canopy, curve right and follow Arroyo Conejo Creek downstream. Cross to the west bank of the stream, and follow the unpaved road lined with stately oaks. Rock hop over the creek two more times to the water treatment plant. Cross the creek and skirt around the left side of the facility on a dirt road. At the north end of the industrial mecca, watch for the first footpath on the right. Take this path, parallel the fenceline, and cross the bridge over the North Fork of Arroyo Conejo Creek. Reenter the beautiful canyon along the north bank of the creek on the Wildwood Canyon Trail. Pass a junction with the Eagle Point Trail, which crosses the creek to the Skunk Hollow Picnic Area. Make two consecutive creek crossings to a junction with the Teepee Trail on the left. Stay to the right towards Paradise Falls, crossing to the south side of the creek. Stroll through an oak grove, and cross to the north side of the creek as Paradise Falls comes into view. Steps to the right lead down to the falls and pool (back cover photo). On the main trail, steps lead up to the brink of the falls, then parallel the cascading creek upstream to a 4-way junction with the Teepee and Lynnmere Trails. Bear right, crossing the creek on the Lynnmere Trail, and ascend the south canyon wall. Forty yards before reaching the Lynnmere Trailhead

HIKES 59 • 60

WILDWOOD PARK

LYNNMERE—WILDWOOD CANYON LOOPS

gate, bear right and traverse the hillside along the south park boundary. Follow the ridge and descend to a junction. Bear left into a draw. Climb up the hill and follow the fenceline to the right, completing the loop.

N
W — E
S

MOUNTCLEF RIDGE

CAMINO DE CELESTE

WILDWOOD AVE

WILDWOOD

63

SANTA ROSA TRAIL

WILDWOOD PARK

BIG SKY DR

SUNDANCE

OLSEN ROAD

MESA TRAIL

62

AVENIDA DE LOS ARBOLES

STAGECOACH BLUFF TRAIL

61

TEEPEE TR.

CANYON TRAIL

EAGLE PT.

Paradise Falls

North Fork

Arroyo Conejo

59

AVENIDA DE LAS

FLORES

SIDLEE

60

TRAIL

LYNNMERE TRAIL

LYNN ROAD

LYNNMERE DRIVE

WATERTOWN COURT

JANSS ROAD

LYNNMERE

START HIKE 60

P

CALLE YUCCA

START HIKE 59

P

ALSO SEE MAP ON PAGE 114

CALLE MANZANAS

TO HWY 101

Hike 61
Paradise Falls
WILDWOOD PARK

Hiking distance: 3 miles round trip
Hiking time: 1.5 hours
Elevation gain: 400 feet
Maps: U.S.G.S. Newbury Park
Wildwood Park Trail Guide

Summary of hike: Wildwood Park has two waterfalls. The larger of the two, Paradise Falls, plunges 70 feet down a wall of volcanic rock into a large pool (back cover photo). This loop hike follows Wildwood Canyon along the North Fork of the Arroyo Conejo down to Paradise Falls and Little Falls. The hike returns up Indian Creek Canyon.

Driving directions: From Highway 101 (Ventura Freeway) in Thousand Oaks, exit on Lynn Road and drive 2.5 miles north to Avenida De Los Arboles. Turn left and continue 0.9 miles to the end of the road at Big Sky Drive. Loop around the center median, and park in the trailhead parking lot on the right.

Hiking directions: Take the trail to the east, away from the mountains. Descend wooden steps to the Moonridge and Indian Creek Trail junction. Take the Moonridge Trail along the west side of Wildwood Canyon. Switchbacks lead down into the canyon and across a wooden bridge. Proceed to a service road. After crossing, stay on the Moonridge Trail along the hilly contours to another junction. Take the signed left fork towards Paradise Falls, crossing a small ravine to the Teepee Overlook Trail, a service road. Head left to Teepee Overlook. Proceed along the road for about 100 yards into the canyon to a junction. Take the signed left trail down the steps to Paradise Falls and to the pool at its base.

After exploring the area around the falls and pool, return up the steps. Take the Wildwood Canyon Trail to the right past the brink of the falls. Pass Little Falls and a picnic area. As the trail parallels Indian Creek, cross the creek on a wooden bridge, and take the signed Indian Creek Trail up the canyon to the left. Cross the creek again and ascend the hill to the top. The left fork leads back to the parking lot.

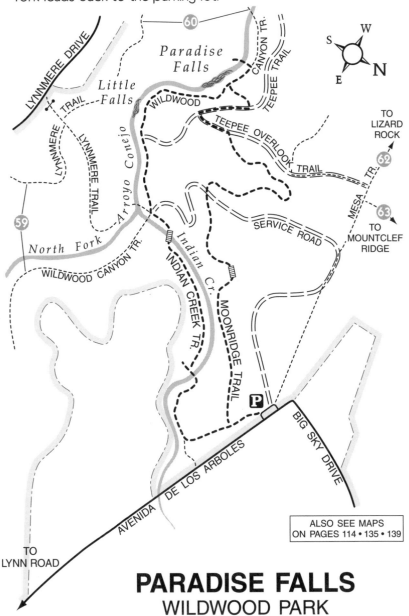

ALSO SEE MAPS
ON PAGES 114 • 135 • 139

PARADISE FALLS
WILDWOOD PARK

Hike 62
Lizard Rock
Mesa—Stagecoach Bluff Loop
WILDWOOD PARK

Hiking distance: 3 miles round trip
Hiking time: 1.5 hours
Elevation gain: 150 feet
Maps: U.S.G.S. Newbury Park
Wildwood Park Trail Guide

Summary of hike: Wildwood Park was the site for numerous television and movie westerns, including *The Rifleman, Bonanza, Wagon Train,* and *Gunsmoke* (and the original town of Dodge City). The hike to Lizard Rock parallels Mountclef Ridge, a serrated volcanic rock outcropping, on an expansive, gently rolling grassland plateau. From the Lizard Rock formations are panoramic views into Box Canyon, Wildwood Canyon, and the surrounding mountains and valleys. The hike returns on the Stagecoach Bluff Trail (named for its numerous stagecoach racing scenes), following the edge of the cliffs 400 feet above Wildwood Canyon.

Driving directions: From Highway 101 (Ventura Freeway) in Thousand Oaks, exit on Lynn Road and drive 2.5 miles north to Avenida De Los Arboles. Turn left and continue 0.9 miles to the end of the road at Big Sky Drive. Loop around the center median, and park in the trailhead parking lot on the right.

Hiking directions: Head west past the trailhead information board and up a short hill. Drop down over the hill to a service road. Follow the road 70 yards to the Mesa Trail, veering off to the right. Take the Mesa Trail across the grasslands, passing the Santa Rosa Trail (Hike 63) and the Teepee Overlook Trail, to a posted trail split. Take the right fork, the Box Canyon Trail, to a knoll. From the knoll, take the left path to the Lizard Rock Trail. Continue along the Lizard Rock Trail to the right. Ascend a short, steep hill to the top of the rock. The trail loops around and rejoins the trail coming up. Retrace your steps to the signed Stagecoach Bluff Trail. Take this trail to the right along the cliff edge overlooking Wildwood Canyon. The trail ends at a junction with the Teepee Overlook Trail. Turn left, rejoining the Mesa Trail 100 yards ahead. Return to the trailhead on the right.

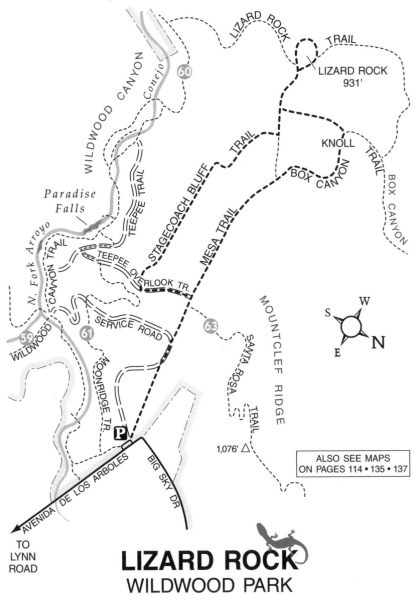

LIZARD ROCK
WILDWOOD PARK

ALSO SEE MAPS
ON PAGES 114 • 135 • 137

Hike 63
Mountclef Ridge
Santa Rosa Trail—Lower Butte Loop
WILDWOOD PARK

Hiking distance: 5 mile loop
Hiking time: 2.5 hours
Elevation gain: 400 feet
Maps: U.S.G.S. Newbury Park
Wildwood Park Trail Guide

Summary of hike: Mountclef Ridge is a volcanic rock out-cropping towering across the northern boundary of Wildwood Park. The Santa Rosa Trail climbs the chaparral clad hillside to the 1,076-foot summit of Mountclef Ridge, traversing the rocky range. From the ridge are great views north across Santa Rosa Valley to the Santa Susana and Topatopa Mountains and south across Conejo Valley to the Santa Monica Mountains.

Driving directions: From Highway 101 (Ventura Freeway) in Thousand Oaks, exit on Lynn Road and drive 2.5 miles north to Avenida De Los Arboles. Turn left and continue 0.9 miles to the end of the road at Big Sky Drive. Loop around the center median, and park in the trailhead parking lot on the right.

Hiking directions: Head west past the trailhead information board and up a short hill. Drop down over the hill to a service road. Follow the road 70 yards to the Mesa Trail, veering off to the right. Take the Mesa Trail across the grasslands to the Santa Rosa Trail on the right. Bear right and head north towards the prominent Mountclef Ridge. The trail traverses the hillside to the east and switchbacks up to the saddle of the Mountclef Ridge summit. Topping the slope, curve right along the contour of the cliff's ridge. A short distance ahead, the trail drops down along the northern slope. Continue east, past the junction with the Wildwood Avenue access trail, to a service road. Take the road to the right to a residential area. Cross the road and continue straight ahead on the signed Lower Butte Trail. Watch for a footpath on the right that leads up to a saddle and over the ridge to the trail's end at Wildwood Avenue. Go left and walk 0.4 miles downhill on the sidewalk to a footpath on the right, across from Sundance Street. Take the path and follow a canal into Wildflower Playfield Park to Avenida De Los Arboles. Complete the loop, returning to the parking lot on the right.

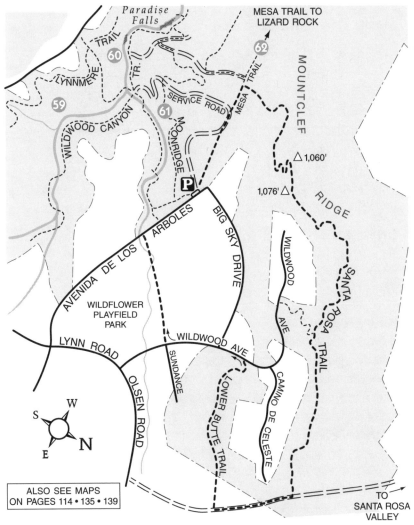

MOUNTCLEF RIDGE
WILDWOOD PARK

Hike 64
Hillcrest Open Space Preserve
NORTH RANCH OPEN SPACE

Hiking distance: 7.2 miles round trip
Hiking time: 3.5 hours
Elevation gain: 600 feet
Maps: U.S.G.S. Thousand Oaks

map
next page

Summary of hikes 64 and 65: The North Ranch Open Space connects the Simi Hills with Thousand Oaks. The Hillcrest Open Space Trail (Hike 64) climbs up an undeveloped canyon in Thousand Oaks. The Sandstone Hills Trail (Hike 65) winds through the Simi Hills among sculpted sandstone formations. The two trails connect at Westlake Boulevard north of Kanan Road. They may be hiked in either direction as a 7.5-mile one-way shuttle. Both trails offer magnificent bird's-eye views of the valley communities and the surrounding mountains.

Driving directions: From Highway 101 (Ventura Freeway) in Thousand Oaks, exit on Westlake Boulevard and drive 1 mile north to Hillcrest Drive. Turn left and drive 0.2 miles to Blue Mesa Street. Turn left and park.

Hiking directions: Walk 0.2 miles west (left) on Hillcrest Drive to the posted trailhead on the north side of the street. Take the path 20 yards to a trail split. Both routes lead up the mountain and join on the ridge. For this hike, take the right fork, which is an easier climb. The trail follows the spine of the hill. Gradually curve left to a flat, round summit with sweeping 360-degree views of the Santa Monica Mountains ridgeline, from Topanga to Point Mugu. Descend to a junction by an open space boundary sign. Bear right and steeply descend to a saddle. Make a horseshoe bend to the right, reaching a knoll by a power pole in the canyon. Traverse the west-facing canyon wall on the fire road while following the contours of the hillside on a gradual uphill grade. The trail makes a steeper ascent for the last quarter mile to the head of the canyon and a

T-junction. The left fork leads to a residential neighborhood west of the canyon. Take the right fork uphill to the ridge. Curve left, descending parallel and above Westlake Boulevard to a junction. Curve sharply to the right 100 yards to Westlake Boulevard. This is our turnaround spot.

For the one-way shuttle hike, cross Westlake Boulevard and walk up Allyson Court. Follow the paved road 0.6 miles to the Sandstone Trail. Continue with Hike 65 in reverse.

Hike 65
Sandstone Hills Trail
NORTH RANCH OPEN SPACE

Hiking distance: 7.8 miles round trip
Hiking time: 4 hours
Elevation gain: 400 feet
Maps: U.S.G.S. Thousand Oaks

map next page

Summary of hike: See previous hike.

Driving directions: From Highway 101 (Ventura Freeway) in Westlake Village, exit on Lindero Canyon Road, and drive 2.9 miles north to Kanan Road. Turn left to the first street—Falling Star Avenue—and turn right. Continue 0.5 miles to Pathfinder Avenue and turn right. Drive one block to the hilltop at the posted Sandstone Hills Trail on the left. Park along the street.

Hiking directions: Walk past the trail gate, and climb a short hill through the wide open space past private residences. Head north towards the jagged sandstone formations below Simi Peak, and ascend a second hill before dropping into an arroyo. At the upper-most hillside home, curve left. Climb wood steps to a power pole and a vista across Westlake Village, Agoura Hills, and the Santa Monica Mountains. Traverse the hillside to the west, parallel to Conejo Ridge. Walk around a chainlink fence to an unpaved fire road. The winding road generally heads west beneath magnificent sandstone formations and caves. At 1.4 miles, a road branches right. Detour to the right 0.6

miles uphill to the outcroppings and caves. Back on the Sandstone Trail, continue 100 yards to a saddle and trail fork. Curve right, crossing over the saddle. The views open up to the west across the valley to the Topatopa Mountains near Ojai and the Santa Monica Mountains at Point Mugu. Descend among the sculpted sandstone rocks, and cross a small grassy meadow at 2.2 miles. Climb out of the valley to another saddle and trail fork. The left fork returns to Kanan Road. Stay to the right 0.1 mile to a 4-way junction. Walk straight ahead on the narrower footpath. Below and to the right is the Albertson Motorway. Follow the ridge, staying left at a Y-fork and heading over the ridge. Cross the rolling grassy hills to a huge water tank on the right and a

ALLYSON COURT

SAPRA ST

GRISSOM

CARPENTER

LA GRANADA DR

ERBES ROAD

64

SKELETON CANYON

WESTLAKE BOULEVARD

TO
MOORPARK AND
SIMI VALLEY

23

HILLCREST DRIVE

△1,581'

TO
VENTURA

START
HIKE 64

P

BLUE MESA

THOUSAND OAKS BOULEVARD

VENTURA FREEWAY

101

N

W E

S

ALSO SEE MAP
ON PAGE 114

TO
LOS ANGELES

paved utility road at 3.3 miles. This is our turnaround spot.

For the one-way shuttle hike, follow the paved road 0.6 miles to Westlake Boulevard at Allyson Court. Cross the road to the gated Hillcrest Open Space entrance. Continue with Hike 64 in reverse.

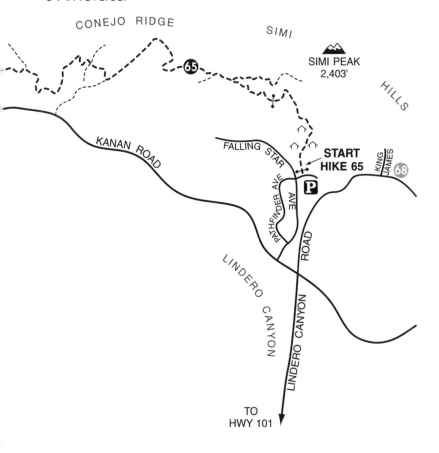

HIKES 64 • 65
NORTH RANCH
OPEN SPACE
HILLCREST OPEN SPACE PRESERVE
SANDSTONE HILLS TRAIL

Hike 66
Oak Canyon Community Park

Hiking distance: 1.6 miles round trip
Hiking time: 45 minutes
Elevation gain: 100 feet
Maps: U.S.G.S. Thousand Oaks

Summary of hike: Oak Canyon Community Park is a beautiful 60-acre park with sandstone cliffs, a year-round creek, and a pond. Medea Creek flows through the length of the park from the south slope of Simi Peak in the Simi Hills. The creek descends from the Conejo Ridge and flows all year, eventually merging with Malibu Creek on its journey to the sea. A nature trail loops through an oak and willow forest with several crossings over Medea Creek. Near the trailhead is a beautiful man-made waterfall cascading into the pond. Walking paths circle the pond.

Driving directions: From Highway 101 (Ventura Freeway) in Agoura Hills, exit on Kanan Road. Head north 3 miles to Hollytree Drive and turn right. Turn left 70 yards ahead into the Oak Canyon Community Park parking lot.

Hiking directions: From the parking lot, take the paved walking path north past the restrooms, playground, and covered picnic area. Follow the curving path up canyon on the east side of Medea Creek and the park road. Various side trails lead down into the oak tree canopy to the willow-lined creek. The trail reaches nature trail station #8 at 0.4 miles. Take the footpath to the left, which leads into the forest to Medea Creek. The trail begins down the canyon and crosses the creek three times. After the third crossing, by station #15, is a junction. The right fork is a quarter-mile side trip through chaparral to an archery range at the back of a small canyon. The left fork leads back to the pond and the trailhead. Several paths cross the creek to the parking lot, or you may circle around the pond.

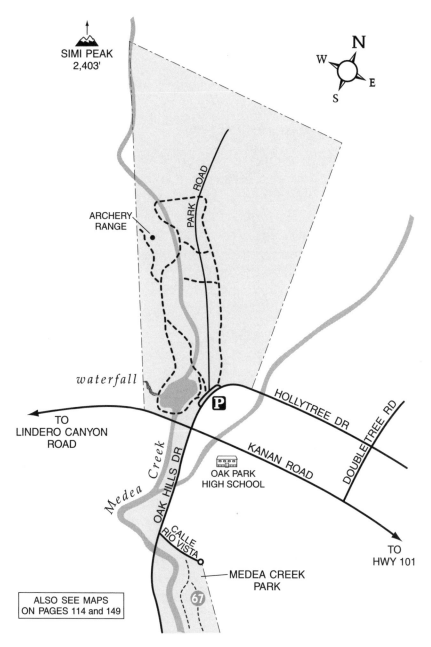

SIMI PEAK
2,403'

N
W   E
S

ARCHERY
RANGE

PARK ROAD

waterfall

TO
LINDERO CANYON
ROAD

P

HOLLYTREE DR

DOUBLETREE RD

KANAN ROAD

OAK PARK
HIGH SCHOOL

Medea Creek

OAK HILLS DR

CALLE
RIO VISTA

TO
HWY 101

MEDEA CREEK
PARK

67

ALSO SEE MAPS
ON PAGES 114 and 149

OAK CANYON
COMMUNITY PARK

Hike 67
Medea Creek Park

Hiking distance: 1.8 miles round trip
Hiking time: 1 hour
Elevation gain: Level
Maps: U.S.G.S. Thousand Oaks

Summary of hike: The Medea Creek Trail winds through Medea Creek Park, an oak-shaded suburban greenbelt in Oak Park. The long and narrow wetland winds through residential neighborhoods, creating a wildlife habitat and urban wilderness. Medea Creek forms on the south flank of Simi Peak in the Simi Hills. The creek descends from Conejo Ridge and flows year-round through Oak Canyon Community Park (Hike 66), Oak Park, Agoura Hills, and into the Santa Monica Mountains, merging with Malibu Creek at Malibu Lake.

Driving directions: From Highway 101 (Ventura Freeway) in Westlake Village, exit on Lindero Canyon Road, and drive 2.9 miles north to Kanan Road. Turn right and drive 1.2 miles to Oak Hills Drive. Turn right and continue 0.2 miles to Calle Rio Vista. Turn left and park in the cul-de-sac.

Hiking directions: Take the paved path southeast 40 yards, skirting the ball fields to a side path on the right. Both paths parallel the stream, but the right fork is a natural path that drops down to the creek, shaded with oaks and willows. Follow the creek downstream, rejoining the paved path. Cross Medea Creek Lane, 90 yards north of Oak Hills Drive, to a T-junction. The left fork returns to Kanan Road by Sunnycrest Drive. Go to the right and cross Oak Hills Drive, just west of Park View Drive, and follow the watercourse. A footpath follows the creek bank, paralleling the paved path. Cross the cement spillway over Medea Creek, and walk through the creekside tunnel under Conifer Street. Cross a long footbridge over Medea Creek to the cul-de sac on East Tamarind Street at the Los Angeles–Ventura county line. From the cul-de-sac, loop back along the east bank of the creek. It is easy to switch from the paved trail to the dirt footpaths and from one side of the creek to the other. Create your own route.

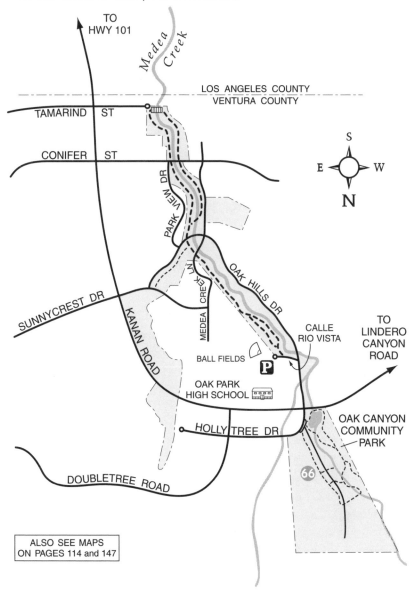

MEDEA CREEK PARK

Hike 68
China Flat Trail
CHEESEBORO/PALO COMADO CANYONS

Hiking distance: 4 mile loop
Hiking time: 2 hours
Elevation gain: 1,000 feet
Maps: U.S.G.S. Thousand Oaks
N.P.S. Cheeseboro/Palo Comado Canyons

Summary of hike: China Flat, a newer addition to the Cheeseboro/Palo Comado Canyons site, is a high, oak-dotted grassland meadow with sedimentary rock outcroppings. The flat is perched on the west side of Palo Comado Canyon beneath the shadows of Simi Peak, the highest peak in the Simi Hills. The China Flat Trail is a steep hike with awesome, panoramic views of Simi Valley, Oak Park, Agoura Hills, and Westlake Village. Connector trails link China Flat to the upper reaches of Palo Comado and Cheeseboro Canyons (Hikes 69 and 70).

Driving directions: From Highway 101 (Ventura Freeway) in Westlake Village, exit on Lindero Canyon Road. Drive 4 miles north and park on Lindero Canyon Road by the China Flat Trailhead on the left. It is located between King James Court and Wembly Avenue.

Hiking directions: Hike north past the trailhead sign towards the mountains. Climb the short, steep hill to where a trail from King James Court merges with the main trail. Continue around the east side of a large sandstone outcropping. The trail levels out and heads east, following the contours of the mountain base, to an unsigned junction. Take the left fork north, heading uphill towards the ridge. Once over the ridge, the trail meets another unsigned junction. Take the left fork and head west, with views overlooking the canyon. Proceed uphill along the ridgeline to a flat area and trail junction. The right fork leads back towards Palo Comado and Cheeseboro Canyons. Take the left fork and descend to another junction. Again, take the left fork, winding downhill to a gate at King James Court. Leave the trail and walk one block on the sidewalk to Lindero Canyon Road. The trailhead is on the left.

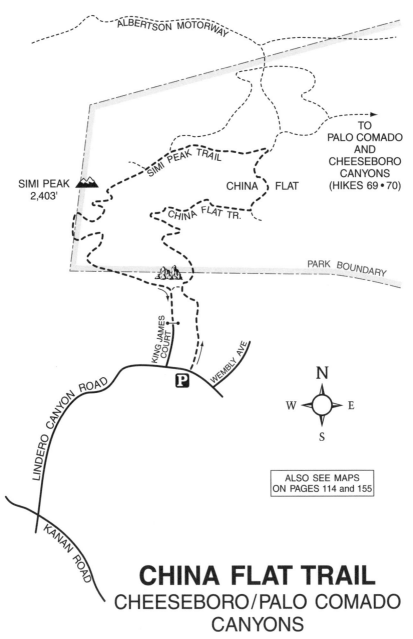

CHINA FLAT TRAIL
CHEESEBORO/PALO COMADO CANYONS

Hike 69
Palo Comado—Cheeseboro Canyons Loop
CHEESEBORO/PALO COMADO CANYONS

Hiking distance: 5 mile loop
Hiking time: 2.5 hours
Elevation gain: 800 feet
Maps: U.S.G.S. Thousand Oaks and Calabasas
N.P.S. Cheeseboro/Palo Comado Canyons

Summary of hike: Palo Comado and Cheeseboro Canyons, in the Simi Hills near Agoura Hills, is a wildlife corridor connecting the Santa Monica Mountains with the Santa Susana Mountains. The north-south corridor allows animals to move between the two ranges. This loop hike heads up the undeveloped Palo Comado Canyon parallel to a stream and meadows. After crossing over into Cheeseboro Canyon, the hike follows the canyon floor on an old ranch road across grasslands with groves of stately valley oaks and twisted coast live oaks.

Driving directions: From Highway 101 (Ventura Freeway) in Agoura Hills, exit on Kanan Road. Head north 2.2 miles to Sunnycrest Drive and turn right. Continue 0.8 miles to the "Public Open Space" sign on the right. Park along the curb.

Hiking directions: From the trailhead, hike east past the gate and up a short hill on the Sunnycrest Connector Trail. As you top the hill, the trail descends into Palo Comado Canyon. Cross the stream at the canyon floor to a junction with the Palo Comado Canyon Trail, an old ranch road. Head left up the canyon through rolling grasslands with sycamore and oak groves. At one mile the trail begins to climb out of the canyon, winding along the contours of the mountain. Near the head of the canyon, the Palo Comado Canyon Trail curves left, heading to China Flat (Hike 68). There is an unmarked but distinct path leading sharply to the right at the beginning of this curve—the Old Sheep Corral Trail. Take this path uphill to a couple of ridges that overlook Cheeseboro Canyon. Descend into the canyon a short distance to the corral and a junction at Shepherds' Flat. Straight ahead the trail climbs up to Cheeseboro Ridge. Take the right fork and follow Cheeseboro Canyon gently downhill. At Sulphur Springs, identified by its smell, walk beneath the white, sedimentary cliffs of the Baleen Wall on the east canyon wall. Continue down canyon through oak groves to the posted Ranch Center Connector Trail, 1.3 miles down the canyon on the right. Bear right and wind 1.1 mile up and over the chaparral hillside from Cheeseboro Canyon back to Palo Comado Canyon. Bear right a short distance, completing the loop. Return to the left on the Sunnycrest Connector Trail.

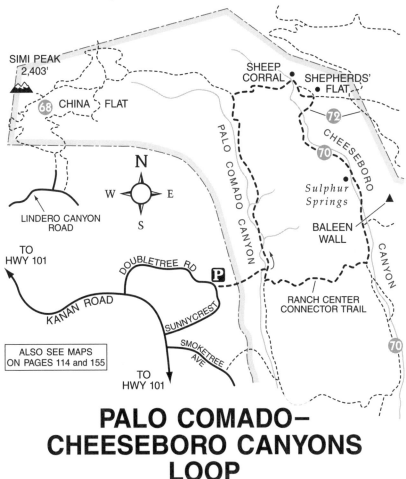

PALO COMADO–
CHEESEBORO CANYONS
LOOP

Hike 70
Cheeseboro Canyon to Shepherds' Flat
CHEESEBORO/PALO COMADO CANYONS

Hiking distance: 8.6 miles round trip
Hiking time: 4 hours
Elevation gain: 600 feet
Maps: U.S.G.S. Calabasas
N.P.S. Cheeseboro/Palo Comado Canyons

Summary of hike: Cheeseboro Canyon is a lush stream-fed canyon with large valley oaks, gnarled coast live oaks, and sycamores. The hike follows an old abandoned ranch road on a gentle grade up the forested canyon bottom. The trail passes fragrant Sulphur Springs as you pass beneath the Baleen Wall, a vertical rock formation on the east canyon wall. At the upper reaches of the canyon is Shepherds' Flat, a grassland flat and a sheep corral.

Driving directions: From Highway 101 (Ventura Freeway) in Agoura Hills, exit on Chesebro Road. Continue one block straight ahead, past the stop sign, to Palo Comado Canyon Road and turn left. Drive 0.3 miles to Chesebro Road again and turn right. Continue 0.7 miles to Cheeseboro Canyon Road and turn right. The trailhead parking lot is 0.2 miles ahead.

Hiking directions: Take the service road east toward Cheeseboro Canyon to a road split. Bear left on the Cheeseboro Canyon Trail, heading into the canyon past the Modelo Trail and the Canyon View Trail. At 1.3 miles is a junction with the Cheeseboro Ridge Connector Trail (also known as the Baleen Wall Trail). Take the left fork towards Sulphur Springs to another junction with the Modelo Trail on the left. Proceed a short distance on the main trail to a junction. Take the left branch. As you near Sulphur Springs, the white, jagged cliffs of the Baleen Wall can be seen towering on the cliffs to the east. At 3.5 miles, the canyon and trail both narrow as the smell of sulphur becomes stronger. At the head of the canyon is a three-way junction at Shepherds' Flat, the turnaround point. Return back to the Modelo Trail junction. Take the Modelo Trail along the western ridge of the canyon back to the trailhead.

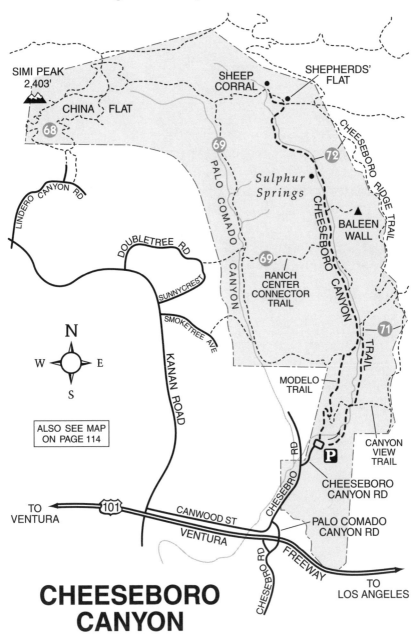

CHEESEBORO CANYON

Hike 71
Canyon View—Cheeseboro Canyon Loop
CHEESEBORO/PALO COMADO CANYONS

Hiking distance: 4 mile loop
Hiking time: 2 hours
Elevation gain: 500 feet
Maps: U.S.G.S. Calabasas
  N.P.S. Cheeseboro/Palo Comado Canyons

Summary of hike: The Canyon View Trail climbs the east wall of Cheeseboro Canyon to a knoll overlooking Cheeseboro Canyon and the Lost Hills landfill. The Cheeseboro Canyon Trail is an abandoned ranch road that passes through groves of 200-year old valley oaks, largest of the California oaks. This hike follows the ridge separating Cheeseboro Canyon from Las Virgenes Canyon, then drops back down to the shaded oak park lands and picnic areas on the canyon floor.

Driving directions: Same as Hike 70.

Hiking directions: Take the well-marked Cheeseboro Canyon Trail, and hike through the rolling hills filled with groves of stately oaks. Pass the Modelo Trail on the left to a posted junction with the Canyon View Trail at a half mile. Bear right, leaving the canyon floor, and climb the grassy canyon hillside. At 0.9 miles, the Canyon View Trail ends at a T-junction and a trail gate on Cheeseboro Ridge. Pass through the gate. The right fork leads 0.3 miles to an overlook of the canyon. Bear left (north) on the Cheeseboro Ridge Trail. Follow the ridge uphill, enjoying the great canyon views, to a Y-fork. Stay left on the undulating ridge, passing power poles. Slowly descend to the Las Virgenes Connector Trail on the right. Stay left 120 yards to the Cheeseboro Canyon Connector Trail on the left. The Cheeseboro Ridge Trail—Hike 72—continues straight ahead along the ridge to Shepherds' Flat. Bear left and descend 0.7 miles down the grass and sage covered hillside to the canyon floor and a picnic area. Bear left on the Cheeseboro Canyon

Trail, an old ranch road, and stroll through the oak groves, completing the loop at the Canyon View Trail junction. Return down-canyon to the trailhead.

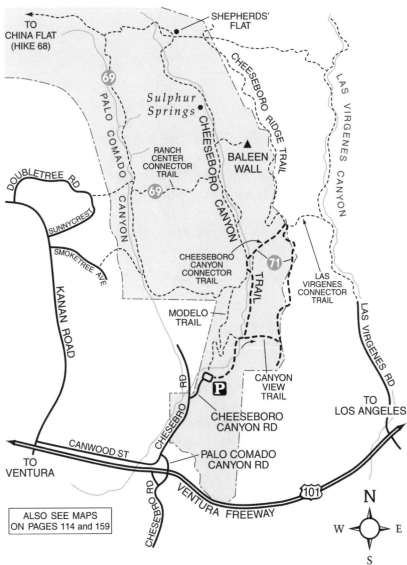

CANYON VIEW–
CHEESEBORO CANYON

Hike 72
Cheeseboro Ridge—
Cheeseboro Canyon Loop
CHEESEBORO/PALO COMADO CANYONS

Hiking distance: 10 mile loop
Hiking time: 5 hours
Elevation gain: 900 feet
Maps: U.S.G.S. Calabasas
N.P.S. Cheeseboro/Palo Comado Canyons

Summary of hike: The Cheeseboro Ridge Trail follows the ridge separating Cheeseboro Canyon and Las Virgenes Canyon in the Simi Hills above Agoura. From the ridge are bird's-eye views into both canyons that extend to the Santa Monica Mountains and across the San Fernando Valley. The hike returns through the shaded oak savannah following the stream through Cheeseboro Canyon.

Driving directions: Same as Hike 70.

Hiking directions: Follow the hiking directions of Hike 71 on the Cheeseboro Ridge Trail to the junction with the Cheeseboro Canyon Connector Trail. Stay to the right (north) on the old ranch road. Wind up the ridge and skirt around the right side of a water tank. Gradually descend to the canyon floor and a trail split. Curve left and head west along the base of the mountain to a signed junction at Shepherds' Flat. The Sheep Corral Trail continues straight ahead to China Flat (Hike 68) and Palo Comado Canyon (Hike 69). Bear left on the Cheeseboro Canyon Trail (also called Sulphur Springs Trail), and follow the canyon floor steadily downhill. At Sulphur Springs, easily identified by its smell, walk beneath the white sedimentary cliffs of the Baleen Wall on the east canyon wall. Continue down canyon through oak groves and past shaded picnic areas. Pass the Ranch Center Connector Trail and the Palo Comado Connector Trail on the right, completing the loop at the Canyon View Trail junction. Return down canyon to the trailhead.

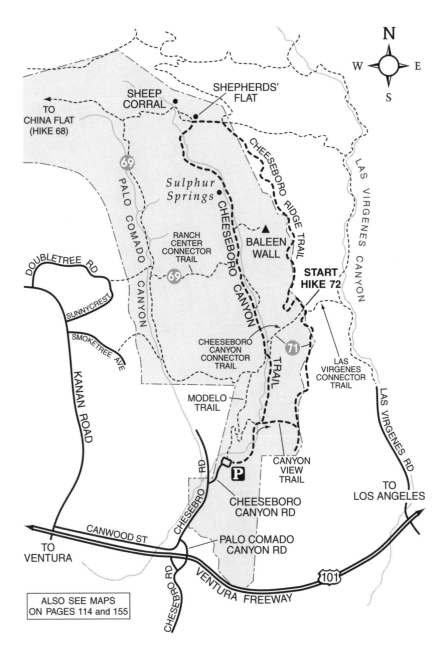

CHEESEBORO RIDGE–
CHEESEBORO CANYON

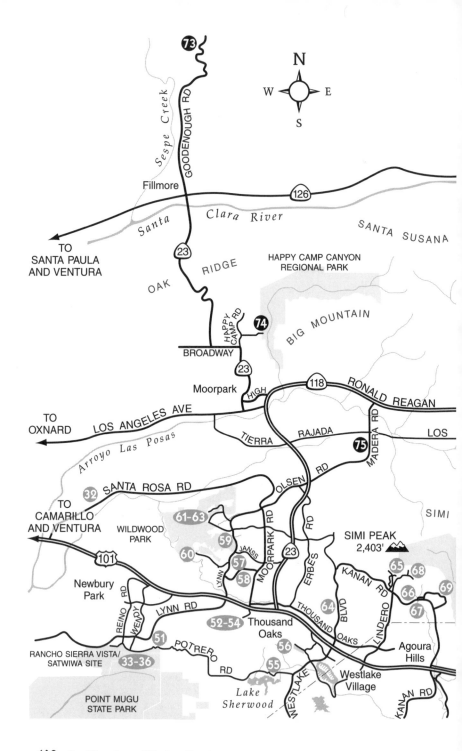

MOUNTAINS

LOS ANGELES COUNTY
VENTURA COUNTY

⑤

GOLDEN STATE FREEWAY

TO
LOS ANGELES

ROCKY
PEAK
76 PARK

77

SANTA SUSANA
PASS ROAD

FREEWAY

YOSEMITE

KUEHNER

78

118

ANGELES AVE

79

80 DEVONSHIRE

SAN DIEGO FREEWAY

Simi Valley

BOX CANYON

PLUMMER

SAN FERNANDO
VALLEY

*Chatsworth
Reservoir*

81

HILLS

WOOLSEY
CANYON RD

VALLEY CIRCLE BLVD

ROSCOE

82

TOPANGA CANYON BLVD

405

Los Angeles River

CHEESEBORO/
PALO COMADO
CANYONS SITE

VENTURA FREEWAY

VENTURA BLVD

TO
LOS ANGELES

70-72

101

LAS VIRGENES

MONICA MTNS

MULHOLLAND HWY

MULHOLLAND DRIVE

SANTA

Hike 73
Tar Creek

Hiking distance: 4 miles round trip
Hiking time: 2 hours
Elevation gain: 700 feet
Maps: U.S.G.S. Fillmore
　　　　Sespe Wilderness Trail Map
　　　　Los Padres National Forest Trail Map

Summary of hike: Tar Creek is in the Los Padres National Forest and the Sespe Condor Sanctuary, a reintroduction area for the California Condor. The creek flows through a grotto of sculptured, sandstone boulders with smooth, water-filled bowls and mossy rocks. This hike follows a well-defined but lightly used trail, descending into a deep canyon to Tar Creek. The trail meanders along the stream to pools, cascades, and waterfalls. A mile downstream, Tar Creek joins with Sespe Creek.

Driving directions: From the town of Fillmore, take A Street (Highway 23) one mile north to Goodenough Road. Turn right and continue 2.7 miles to Squaw Flat Road on the right. It is marked as the Dough Flat turnoff. Turn right and drive 4.8 miles up the winding mountain road to the unsigned parking pullout on the left. It is located 1.5 miles beyond the Oak Flat Guard Station.

Hiking directions: From the parking area, take the wide path northwest past the metal gate. The trail winds around the mountainside, with views of the surrounding mountains and the canyon below. As the trail begins its descent, the path narrows to a single track. At the final descent, the trail overlooks Tar Creek. Once at the creek, explore up and down the stream. There are more waterfalls and pools downstream, but the hike becomes demanding and technical. After enjoying the creek, return along the same path.

To hike further, head upstream and curve away from Tar

Creek. The trail weaves along the contours of Sulphur Peak, reaching Sespe Creek in 3 miles.

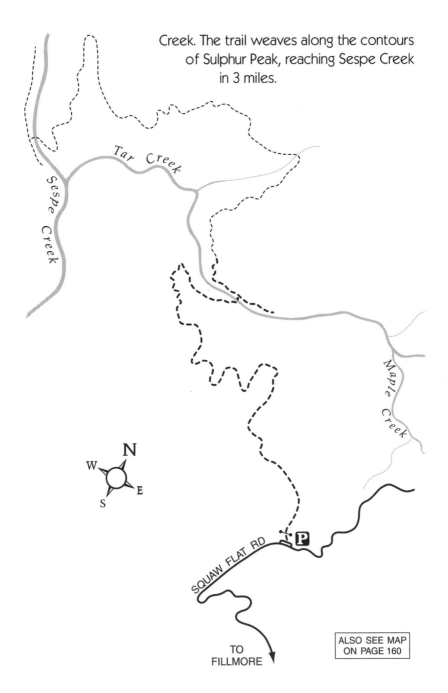

Tar Creek

Sespe Creek

Maple Creek

N
W   E
S

SQUAW FLAT RD

P

TO FILLMORE

ALSO SEE MAP
ON PAGE 160

TAR CREEK

Hike 74
Happy Camp Canyon

Hiking distance: 10 miles round trip
Hiking time: 5 hours
Elevation gain: 1,300 feet
Maps: U.S.G.S. Simi Valley West

Summary of hike: Happy Camp Canyon Park, north of Moorpark in the Santa Susana Mountains, was once part of a large cattle ranch. The 3,000-acre park has retained its natural setting and is an important wildlife corridor linking the Simi Hills with the Santa Susana Mountains. Happy Camp Canyon is a lush riparian oak woodland with an intermittent stream. The canyon is sheltered by Oak Ridge to the north and Big Mountain to the south. The remote park has miles of hiking, biking, and equestrian trails. This hike follows the Happy Camp Trail through the interior of the park on an abandoned ranch road. The trail winds through open grasslands and the gorgeous stream-fed canyon.

Driving directions: From the town of Moorpark, take Moorpark Avenue (Highway 23) 2.5 miles north to a sharp left bend in the road. (Moorpark Avenue becomes Walnut Canyon Road en route.) Continue straight ahead 30 yards on Happy Camp Road to Broadway and turn right. Drive 0.3 miles to the Happy Camp Canyon parking lot at the road's end.

Hiking directions: Overlooking the valley, the trail heads downhill past the trailhead sign. Cross the hillside to the grassy valley floor, joining the old ranch road at one mile. Turn left up canyon a quarter mile to the Happy Camp Canyon Nature Trail kiosk. One hundred yards beyond the kiosk is a trail split. The right fork heads up Big Mountain, the return route. Take the left fork and begin the loop, curving east into the shady canyon. Parallel the stream, then walk across it. At 3.5 miles is the first of several road forks. The left (north) forks are powerline maintenance roads. Take the right fork each time, staying in the canyon. At 4.5 miles, the trail passes a gate, entering an oak grove with picnic tables and horse corrals. Continue east to a junction. Take the steep, half-mile trail to the right, gaining 600 feet to the ridge of Big Mountain. Return along the ridge road to the right, overlooking Happy Camp Canyon and the surrounding mountains. Descend to the valley floor and complete the loop near the kiosk. Return to the left.

BIG MOUNTAIN

OAK RIDGE

N E S W

HAPPY CAMP CANYON
REGIONAL PARK

KIOSK

P

CAMP CANYON

HAPPY

BROADWAY

TO
MOORPARK

ALSO SEE MAP
ON PAGE 160

HAPPY CAMP RD

23

MOORPARK AVE

BROADWAY ROAD

HAPPY CAMP
CANYON

Hike 75
Mount McCoy

Hiking distance: 2.6 miles round trip
Hiking time: 1.5 hours
Elevation gain: 600 feet
Maps: U.S.G.S. Simi Valley West

Summary of hike: Mount McCoy is an isolated 600-foot knoll in a 200-acre open space at the west end of Simi Valley. A white, concrete cross, erected in 1941, sits atop the 1,325-foot summit and is a visible landmark throughout the valley. The wide trail to the summit is composed of a series of switchbacks for an easy, gradual climb. From the summit are 360-degree panoramas of Simi Valley, the Ronald Reagan Presidential Library, the Santa Susana Mountains, the Conejo Ridge, the San Gabriel Mountains, and the Santa Monica Mountains. It was engineered and is maintained by the Rancho Simi Trail Blazers.

Driving directions: From Highway 118 (Ronald Reagan Freeway) in Simi Valley, take the Madera Road South exit. Drive 1.6 miles south to Royal Avenue and turn right. Immediately turn right on Acapulco Avenue, then quickly turn left on Washburn Street. Drive one block to the end of the street at the junction with Los Amigos Avenue. Park near the trailhead on the left.

Hiking directions: From the trailhead, an old steep path heads nearly straight up the east flank of the mountain. For a longer but more enjoyable hike, take the new, lower path to the left, skirting the base of Mount McCoy across the grasslands. Cross to the south side of the drainage filled with coastal live oaks. Ascend the slope on a series of long, sweeping switchbacks through coastal sage scrub and chaparral. The northern switchbacks skirt the edge of the oak studded canyon, but the trail never enters the shaded canopy. Cross over volcanic rock to an old dirt road on the ridgeline. To the left, the dirt road leads to the Ronald Reagan Presidential Library. Take the route to the right, soon merging with the steep, direct route. At 100

yards, the path reaches the concrete cross at the summit. After
taking in the views, return on the same path.

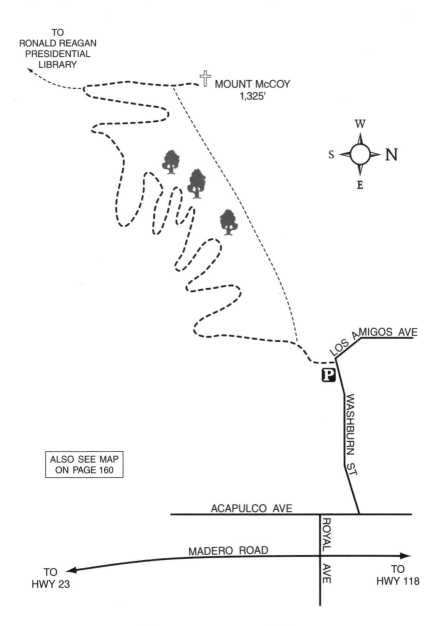

TO
RONALD REAGAN
PRESIDENTIAL
LIBRARY

✝ MOUNT McCOY
1,325'

W
S ⊙ N
E

LOS AMIGOS AVE

🅿

WASHBURN ST

ALSO SEE MAP
ON PAGE 160

ACAPULCO AVE

ROYAL AVE

MADERO ROAD

TO
HWY 23

TO
HWY 118

MOUNT McCOY

Hike 76
Chumash Trail
ROCKY PEAK PARK

Hiking distance: 5 miles round trip
Hiking time: 2.5 hours
Elevation gain: 1,100 feet
Maps: U.S.G.S. Simi Valley East

Summary of hike: The Chumash Trail ascends the west flank of Rocky Peak in the Santa Susana Mountains east of Simi Valley. The trail winds up the chaparral cloaked mountainside to the ridge north of Rocky Peak, passing sculpted sandstone outcroppings, caves, and a series of scenic overlooks and highland meadows. From Hamilton Saddle and the Rocky Peak Trail junction are panoramic views of the Simi Hills, Simi Valley, San Fernando Valley, the Santa Susana Mountains, the Santa Monica Mountains, Blind Canyon, and Las Llajas Canyon.

Driving directions: From Highway 118 (Ronald Reagan Freeway) in Simi Valley, exit on Yosemite Avenue. Drive 0.4 miles north to Flanagan Drive and turn right. Continue 0.8 miles to the trailhead at the end of the road.

Hiking directions: Head north past the kiosk along the rolling hills and grassy meadows. The trail climbs steadily as you round the hillside to the first overlook of the Simi Hills to the south. The trail continues uphill through coastal sage scrub, curving left around the next rolling hill. The trail passes sculpted sandstone formations. Arrow signposts are placed along the route. Continue to the east along the edge of the canyon to Hamilton Saddle. From the saddle, the trail sharply curves left (north), gaining elevation before leveling out again at Flat Rock. From Flat Rock, the trail begins its final ascent through chaparral, curving around the last ridge to the top. The trail ends at a junction with the Rocky Peak Trail at an elevation of 2,450 feet. Sixty yards to the left of the junction are views of Blind Canyon and Las Llajas Canyon. Reverse your route to return.

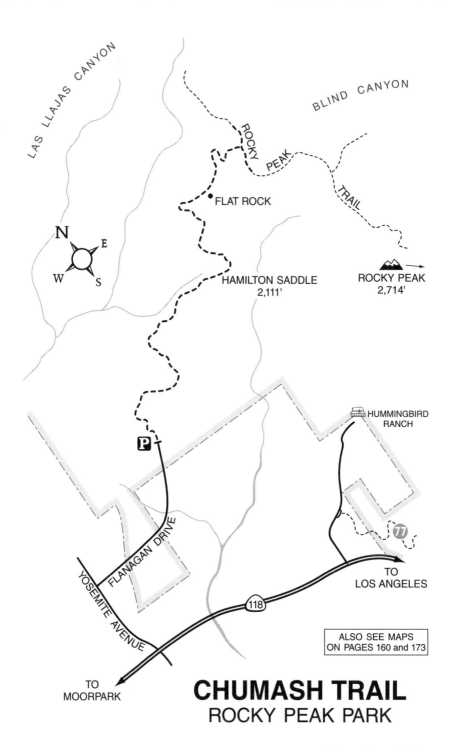

LAS LLAJAS CANYON

BLIND CANYON

ROCKY PEAK TRAIL

•FLAT ROCK

N
E
W
S

HAMILTON SADDLE
2,111'

ROCKY PEAK
2,714'

HUMMINGBIRD
RANCH

P

77

FLANAGAN DRIVE

TO
LOS ANGELES

YOSEMITE AVENUE

118

ALSO SEE MAPS
ON PAGES 160 and 173

TO
MOORPARK

CHUMASH TRAIL
ROCKY PEAK PARK

Hike 77
Hummingbird Trail
ROCKY PEAK PARK

Hiking distance: 4.6 miles round trip
Hiking time: 2 hours
Elevation gain: 1,000 feet
Maps: U.S.G.S. Simi Valley East

Summary of hike: Rocky Peak Park in the Santa Susana Mountains straddles the Los Angeles—Ventura county line at the eastern end of Simi Valley. A network of hiking trails weaves through the 4,815-acre park that is home to deep oak-lined canyons, trickling streams, and massive, sculpted sandstone formations with a moonscape appearance. The Hummingbird Trail, at the base of Rocky Peak, crosses Hummingbird Creek and climbs up a narrow canyon through open chaparral to the Rocky Peak Fire Road, passing stacks of giant sandstone boulders, sculpted caves, and dramatic rock outcroppings.

Driving directions: From Highway 118 (Ronald Reagan Freeway) in Simi Valley, exit on Kuehner Drive. Drive 0.3 miles north to the signed trailhead on the right. Park in one of the pullouts alongside the road. If full, additional parking is available just north of the freeway.

Hiking directions: From the trailhead kiosk, head downhill to the north. The trail soon U-turns southeast into the canyon to a defunct rock dam from 1917 and Hummingbird Creek. Proceed past the dam into an oak woodland and meadow. Once past the meadow, the trail crosses Hummingbird Creek and begins the ascent up the mountain through chaparral. Switchbacks lead up to sandstone caves and rock formations. After the rocks and caves, the trail levels out before the second ascent. Switchbacks make the climb easier as it heads up the canyon. At the head of the canyon, the trail levels out and passes more rock formations. The trail ends at a junction with the Rocky Peak Trail—Hike 78. Return to the trailhead by retracing your steps.

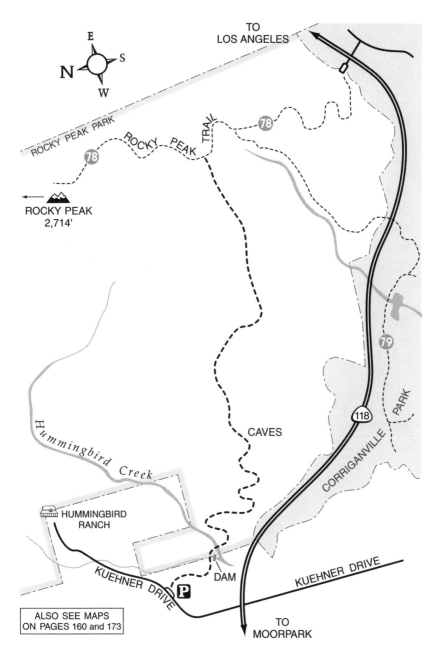

TO
LOS ANGELES

E
N S
W

ROCKY PEAK PARK

ROCKY PEAK TRAIL

78

78

ROCKY PEAK
2,714'

78

79

118

CORRIGANVILLE PARK

CAVES

Hummingbird Creek

HUMMINGBIRD
RANCH

KUEHNER DRIVE

DAM

KUEHNER DRIVE

P

ALSO SEE MAPS
ON PAGES 160 and 173

TO
MOORPARK

HUMMINGBIRD TRAIL
ROCKY PEAK PARK

Hike 78
Rocky Peak Trail
ROCKY PEAK PARK

Hiking distance: 5–6 miles round trip
Hiking time: 2.5 hours
Elevation gain: 1,100 feet
Maps: U.S.G.S. Simi Valley East

Summary of hike: Rocky Peak Park is aptly named for the dramatic sandstone formations, fractured boulders, overhangs, and outcroppings. The 4,815-acre wilderness park is located in Simi Valley by Santa Susana Pass. The park is a critical wildlife habitat linkage between the Simi Hills and the Santa Susana Mountains. Rocky Peak Trail follows a winding fire road on the north side of the 118 freeway to Rocky Peak, which lies on the Los Angeles–Ventura county line. There are a series of vista points along the route and at the jagged 2,714-foot peak, including top-of-the-world views of the San Fernando Valley, Simi Valley, the Santa Monica Mountains, and the many peaks of the Los Padres National Forest.

Driving directions: From Highway 118 (Ronald Reagan Freeway) in Simi Valley, exit on Kuehner Drive. Drive 3 miles south to the Highway 118 East on-ramp. (Along the way, Kuehner Drive becomes Santa Susana Pass Road.) Turn left, crossing over the freeway, and park 0.1 mile ahead at the end of the road.

Hiking directions: Hike past the trailhead kiosk up the winding fire road to an unsigned trail split at 0.9 miles. Stay to the left on the main trail, hiking steadily uphill to a signed junction with the Hummingbird Trail on the left (Hike 77). Proceed straight ahead on the Rocky Peak Trail, which levels out. The winding trail offers alternating views of the San Fernando Valley to the east and Simi Valley to the west. At the base of the final ascent is a singular, large oak tree. Begin the steep ascent, gaining 450 feet in a half mile, to the Rocky Peak Cutoff Trail. This is a good turnaround spot.

However, if you wish to hike to the summit, the trail takes off to the right across the plateau for a half mile to Rocky Peak. The last portion is a rock scramble to the peak. To return, reverse your route.

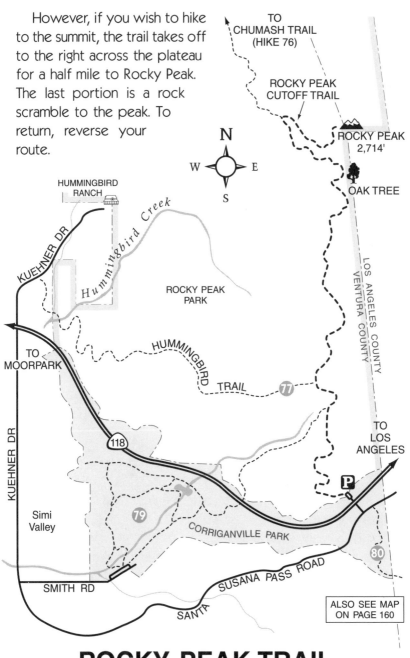

TO
CHUMASH TRAIL
(HIKE 76)

ROCKY PEAK
CUTOFF TRAIL

ROCKY PEAK
2,714'

OAK TREE

N
W E
S

HUMMINGBIRD
RANCH

Hummingbird Creek

KUEHNER DR

ROCKY PEAK
PARK

LOS ANGELES COUNTY
VENTURA COUNTY

TO
MOORPARK

HUMMINGBIRD

TRAIL   77

TO
LOS
ANGELES

KUEHNER DR

118

79

P

Simi
Valley

CORRIGANVILLE PARK

80

SMITH RD

SANTA SUSANA PASS ROAD

ALSO SEE MAP
ON PAGE 160

ROCKY PEAK TRAIL
ROCKY PEAK PARK

Hike 79
Corriganville Park

Hiking distance: 2 miles round trip
Hiking time: 1 hour
Elevation gain: 100 feet
Maps: U.S.G.S. Simi Valley East
        Rancho Simi Open Space: Corriganville Park

Summary of hike: Corriganville Park, at the eastern end of Simi Valley, was an old movie ranch. It was the setting to about a thousand movie and television shows between 1937 and 1965, including *The Lone Ranger, Gunsmoke, The Fugitive, Lassie, Mutiny on the Bounty, African Queen, How The West Was Won,* and *Fort Apache,* to name just a few. Old stone and concrete foundations from the sets still remain. The oak-shaded paths lead through the 225-acre park past prominent sandstone outcroppings, cliffs, caves, a stream, Jungle Jim Lake, and Hangin' Tree, a towering oak used to "execute" countless outlaws.

Driving directions: From Highway 118 (Ronald Reagan Freeway) in Simi Valley, exit on Kuehner Drive. Drive 1.1 mile south to Smith Road and turn left. Continue 0.4 miles into Corriganville Park and park on the left.

Hiking directions: From the far east end of the parking lot, take the wide trail past the kiosk. The forested trail heads northeast up the draw past coast live oaks and sculpted rock formations on the left. Cross a bridge to a junction. The left fork crosses a wooden bridge, passes a pool, and loops back for a short hike. Stay to the right to the next junction. The right fork is a connector trail to Rocky Peak Park (Hike 78) via a concrete tunnel under the freeway. Curve to the left and cross the stream to another junction. Both trails lead west back to the trailhead. The footpath to the right travels between the sandstone cliffs to a dynamic overlook and a junction. Take the left fork, descending to the old movie sets and the site of Fort Apache. From the sets, cross the bridge back to the parking lot.

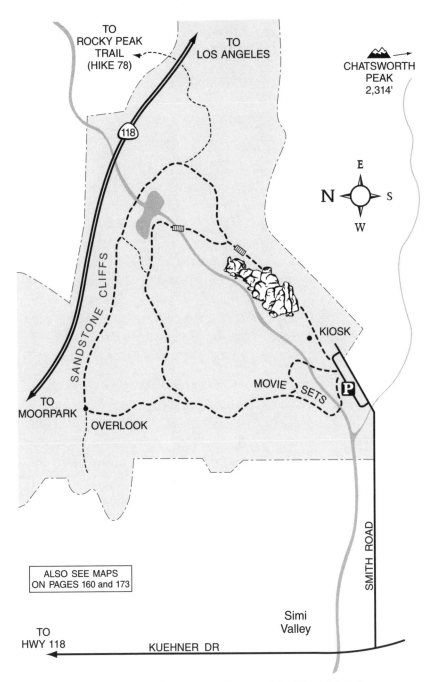

TO
ROCKY PEAK
TRAIL
(HIKE 78)

TO
LOS ANGELES

CHATSWORTH
PEAK
2,314'

E

N ←⊕→ S

W

118

SANDSTONE CLIFFS

KIOSK

MOVIE SETS

P

TO
MOORPARK

OVERLOOK

ALSO SEE MAPS
ON PAGES 160 and 173

SMITH ROAD

Simi
Valley

TO
HWY 118

KUEHNER DR

CORRIGANVILLE PARK

Hike 80
Old Stagecoach Trail

Hiking distance: 2.6 miles round trip
Hiking time: 1.5 hours
Elevation gain: 600 feet
Maps: U.S.G.S. Simi Valley East and Oat Mountain

Summary of hike: The Old Stagecoach Trail begins in Chatsworth Park South and climbs through the undeveloped wilderness of the Santa Susana Mountains. The route follows the historic Santa Susana Stage Road that once linked Los Angeles with San Francisco from 1859—1890. A web of unmarked and confusing trails weaves through rounded, fractured sedimentary rock to vistas of the city of Chatsworth, the San Fernando Valley, and the Santa Susana Mountains. Near the ridge is a plaque embedded into the sandstone rock. The marker was installed by the Native Daughters of the Golden West in 1937, designating the Old Santa Susana Stage Road.

Driving directions: From Highway 118 (Ronald Reagan Freeway) in Chatsworth, take the Topanga Canyon Boulevard exit. Drive 1.5 miles south to Devonshire Street and turn right. Continue a half mile to the end of Devonshire Street and enter Chatsworth Park South. Curve right and drive 0.2 miles to the main parking lot.

From Highway 101 (Ventura Freeway) in Woodland Hills, drive 5 miles north on Topanga Canyon Boulevard to Devonshire Street and turn left.

Hiking directions: Follow the fire road trail on the south (left) edge of Chatsworth Park South, skirting the wide park lawn. At the west end of the open grassland, take a gravel path towards the towering sandstone formations, just below the water tank on the right. Wind up the hillside past large boulders to an old paved road. Take the road 50 yards to the right, and bear left on the dirt path by two telephone poles. Climb to the ridge and a junction surrounded by the sculpted rocks. The left fork loops back to the park. Continue straight 50 yards and curve left towards Devil's Slide, a natural sandstone staircase. Follow the east edge of the chaparral covered slope to an unsigned junction on the left. Bear left and climb the Devil's Slide, stair-stepping up the mountain on the stagecoach-worn bedrock. The sandstone slab leads to a huge rock with a historic plaque cemented into its face. From this overlook is a view into the Santa Susana railroad tunnel and across the San Fernando Valley. A quarter mile beyond the overlook is the 1,630-foot ridge atop the Devil's Slide, near the Los Angeles—Ventura county line. A number of trails wind through the hills and connect to Corriganville Park (Hike 79) and Rocky Peak Park (Hike 78). Return on the same path or explore some of the side trails.

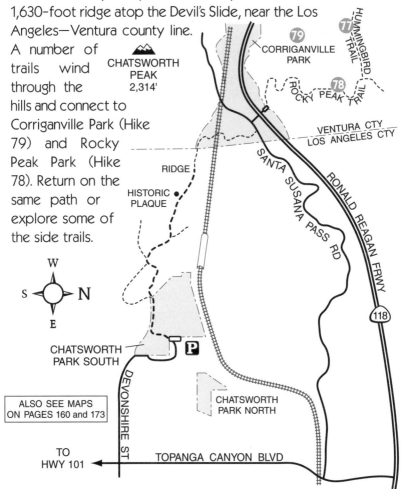

OLD STAGECOACH TRAIL

Hike 81
Sage Ranch Loop Trail

Hiking distance: 2.6 mile loop
Hiking time: 1.3 hours
Elevation gain: 300 feet
Maps: U.S.G.S. Calabasas
        Santa Monica Mountains Conservancy: Sage Ranch Park

Summary of hike: Sage Ranch sits at 2,000 feet and has a garden-of-the-gods appearance. Located in the rocky Simi Hills overlooking the valley, this 635-acre park is rich with world-class sandstone formations. The ranch is an inter-mountain habitat linkage connecting the Simi Hills with the Santa Monica and Santa Susana Mountains. The park boasts an endless display of unique boulders and tilted sandstone outcroppings. Sandstone Ridge, a long, steep, weathered formation with caves and natural sculptures, rises 300 feet from this loop trail. Beautiful carved boulders and eucalyptus trees fill the canyon.

Driving directions: From Highway 118 (Ronald Reagan Freeway) in the San Fernando Valley, exit on Topanga Canyon Boulevard. Drive south and turn right on Plummer Street. Continue 2.4 miles to Woolsey Canyon Road and turn right. (Along the way, Plummer Street becomes Valley Circle Boulevard and Lake Manor Drive.) Continue on Woolsey Canyon Road 2.4 miles to Black Canyon Road and turn right. The Sage Ranch parking lot is 0.2 miles ahead on the left.

From Ventura Freeway (Highway 101) in the San Fernando Valley, exit on Valley Circle Boulevard. Drive north to Woolsey Canyon Road and turn left.

Hiking directions: From the parking lot, hike west up the park service road. Proceed through the gate, passing orange groves on both sides. At the top of the hill next to the sandstone formations, the trail leaves the paved road and takes the gravel road to the right (north). Continue past a meadow dotted with oak trees and through an enormous garden of sandstone rocks. Watch for a short path on the right to a vista point overlooking Simi Valley. Back on the main trail, the trail parallels Sandstone Ridge before descending into the canyon. Once in the canyon, the trail curves back to the east past another series of large rock formations. Near the east end of the canyon is a trail split. Take the left fork, heading uphill and out of the canyon, back to the parking lot.

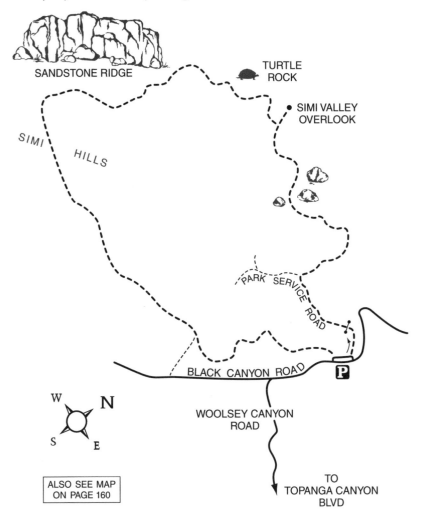

SAGE RANCH LOOP TRAIL

Hike 82
Orcutt Ranch Horticulture Center
23600 Roscoe Boulevard · West Hills
Open daily 8 a.m. to 5 p.m.

Hiking distance: 1 mile round trip
Hiking time: 45 minutes
Elevation gain: Level
Maps: U.S.G.S. Calabasas and Canoga Park
      Orcutt Ranch Horticulture Center map

Summary of hike: Orcutt Ranch Horticulture Center is tucked away at the west end of the San Fernando Valley in West Hills. The 200-acre estate was the vacation home of William and Mary Orcutt, dating back to 1917. The tree-studded estate, designated as a historical monument, was purchased by the Los Angeles Parks and Recreation Department in 1966 and opened to the public. The mission-style home with 16-inch thick adobe walls and a large patio area is nestled under the shade of ancient oaks, including a 700-year-old coastal live oak with a 33-foot circumference. Exotic plants and trees are planted on several acres around the former residence. Amid the fountains and statues are rattan palms, cork oaks, dogwoods, sycamores, birch, bunya bunya trees, purple lily magnolias, Chinese wisterias, bamboo, and a rose garden. An orchard of citrus and walnut groves covers the adjacent rolling hills.

Driving directions: From Highway 118 (Ronald Reagan Freeway) in Chatsworth, take the Topanga Canyon Boulevard exit. Drive 3.2 miles south to Roscoe Boulevard and turn right. Continue 2 miles to the posted park entrance on the left.

From Highway 101 (Ventura Freeway) in Woodland Hills, drive 3.4 miles north on Topanga Canyon Boulevard to Roscoe Boulevard and turn left.

Hiking directions: From the parking area, walk to the Parks and Recreation adobe buildings and the Orcutt estate house. After strolling through the patio areas, take the nature trail into the gardens. Dayton Creek flows through the south end of the gardens in a lush woodland. Along the creek are footbridges, statues, and benches. Design your own route, meandering through the historic estate and gardens.

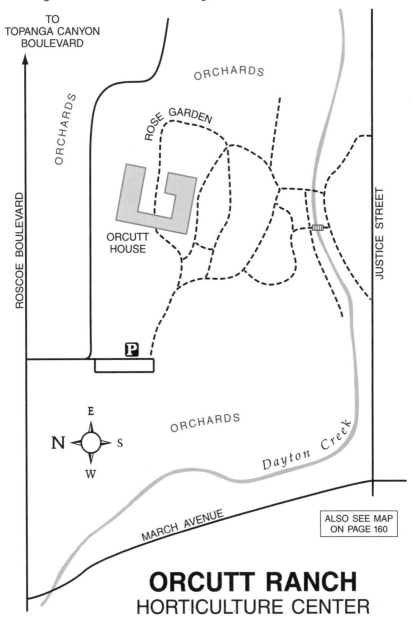

ORCUTT RANCH
HORTICULTURE CENTER

Other Day Hike Guidebooks

Day Hikes On the California Central Coast 14.95

Day Hikes On the California Southern Coast 14.95

Day Hikes Around Monterey and Carmel 14.95

Day Hikes Around Big Sur 14.95

Day Hikes In San Luis Obispo County, California 14.95

Day Hikes Around Santa Barbara 14.95

Day Hikes Around Ventura County 14.95

Day Hikes Around Los Angeles 14.95

Day Hikes In Yosemite National Park 11.95

Day Hikes In Sequoia and Kings Canyon National Parks 12.95

Day Hikes In Yellowstone National Park 9.95

Day Hikes In Grand Teton National Park 11.95

Day Hikes In the Beartooth Mountains
Red Lodge, Montana to Yellowstone National Park 11.95

Day Hikes Around Bozeman, Montana 11.95

Day Hikes Around Missoula, Montana 11.95

Day Hikes On Oahu 11.95

Day Hikes On Maui 11.95

Day Hikes On Kauai 11.95

Day Trips On St. Martin 9.95

Day Hikes In Sedona, Arizona 9.95

These books may be purchased at your local bookstore or
outdoor shop. Or, order them direct from the distributor:

The Globe Pequot Press
246 Goose Lane · P.O. Box 480 · Guilford, CT 06437-0480
www.globe-pequot.com
800-243-0495

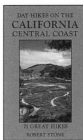

DAY HIKES ON THE
CALIFORNIA
CENTRAL COAST

71 GREAT HIKES
ROBERT STONE

DAY HIKES ON THE
California
Southern
Coast

99 GREAT HIKES
Robert Stone

DAY HIKES AROUND
MONTEREY
& CARMEL

77 GREAT HIKES
ROBERT STONE

DAY HIKES AROUND
BIG SUR

80 GREAT HIKES
ROBERT STONE

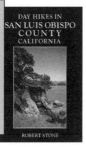

DAY HIKES IN
SAN LUIS OBISPO
COUNTY
CALIFORNIA

ROBERT STONE

DAY HIKES AROUND
SANTA
BARBARA

82 GREAT HIKES
ROBERT STONE

DAY HIKES AROUND
Ventura
County

82 GREAT HIKES
Robert Stone
2nd EDITION

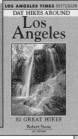

LOS ANGELES TIMES BESTSELLER
DAY HIKES AROUND
Los
Angeles

82 GREAT HIKES
Robert Stone
4th EDITION

DAY HIKES IN
YOSEMITE
NATIONAL PARK

55 GREAT HIKES
ROBERT STONE

DAY HIKES IN
SEQUOIA
AND
KINGS CANYON
NATIONAL PARKS

ROBERT STONE

DAY HIKES IN
YELLOWSTONE
NATIONAL PARK

54 GREAT HIKES
ROBERT STONE

DAY HIKES IN
Grand
Teton
NATIONAL PARK

72 GREAT HIKES
Robert Stone
4th EDITION

DAY HIKES IN THE
BEARTOOTH
MOUNTAINS

RED LODGE, MONTANA TO
YELLOWSTONE NATIONAL PARK
ROBERT STONE

DAY HIKES AROUND
BOZEMAN
MONTANA

INCLUDING THE GALLATIN
CANYON AND PARADISE VALLEY
ROBERT STONE

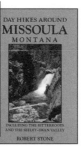

DAY HIKES AROUND
MISSOULA
MONTANA

INCLUDING THE BITTERROOTS
AND THE SEELEY-SWAN VALLEY
ROBERT STONE

DAY HIKES ON
OAHU

57 GREAT HIKES
ROBERT STONE

DAY HIKES ON
MAUI

55 GREAT HIKES
ROBERT STONE

DAY HIKES ON
KAUAI

55 GREAT HIKES
ROBERT STONE

DAY TRIPS ON
ST. MARTIN

ROBERT STONE

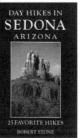

DAY HIKES IN
SEDONA
ARIZONA

25 FAVORITE HIKES
ROBERT STONE

Notes

About the Author

For more than a decade, veteran hiker Robert Stone has been writer, photographer, and publisher of Day Hike Books. Robert resides summers in the Rocky Mountains of Montana and winters on the California Central Coast. This year-round temperate climate enables him to hike throughout the year. When not hiking, Robert is researching, writing, and mapping the hikes before returning to the trails. He is an active member of OWAC (Outdoor Writers Association of California). Robert has hiked every trail in the Day Hike Book series. With over twenty hiking guides in the series, he has hiked over a thousand trails throughout the western United States and Hawaii.